LOOKING FOR *Love* IN THE WRONG PLACE

LOOKING FOR Love IN THE WRONG PLACE

JANNIE WILCOXSON

WINEPRESS WP PUBLISHING

© 2006 by Jannie Wilcoxson. All rights reserved.

Editor: Lisa Rife

WinePress Publishing (PO Box 428, Enumclaw, WA 98022) functions only as book publisher. As such, the ultimate design, content, editorial accuracy, and views expressed or implied in this work are those of the author.

No part of this publication may be reproduced, stored in a retrieval system or transmitted in any way by any means—electronic, mechanical, photocopy, recording or otherwise—without the prior permission of the copyright holder, except as provided by USA copyright law.

Unless otherwise noted, all Scriptures are taken from the New American Standard Bible, © 1960, 1963, 1968, 1971, 1972, 1973, 1975, 1977 by The Lockman Foundation. Used by permission.

Scripture references marked KJV are taken from the King James Version of the Bible.

Scripture references marked NKJV are taken from the New King James Version, © 1979, 1980, 1982 by Thomas Nelson, Inc., Publishers. Used by permission.

ISBN 1-57921-867-9
Library of Congress Catalog Card Number: 2006904564

Printed in Colombia.

CONTENTS

Foreword	vii
1. A Love Triangle	9
2. She Loves Me?	33
3. What's Love Got to Do with It?	49
4. Love Abused	103
5. Blinded by Love	119
6. Love Transforms	145
7. Love Trap	159
8. For the Love of Money	173
9. Bushels of Love	193
Appendix: Absolutely Sure	223
Bibliography	229

Foreword

Where is the love that can reach the depth of your pain and pull you out, soothe, comfort, and embrace you? Love that is always forgiving, yet revealing; always protecting, never pushing away; always patient, never jealous; always kind, never rude, irritable, or touchy. Where is the love that does not demand its own way and never stops loving even when you do not love in return or when you do wrong? Love that will not hold a grudge or keep a record of your errors or mistakes, but always trusts, always hopes, and always perseveres.

In this inductive study, based on the stories of a variety of individuals throughout the Bible, you will discover God's everlasting love, a love that only God can provide, a love that lasts.

—J. WILCOXSON

> Behold [see] what manner of [how great a] love the Father has bestowed [given] on us, that we should be called children of God. —1 John 3:1 (KJV)

Chapter 1

A LOVE TRIANGLE
LEAH, RACHEL, AND JACOB

A man…a woman…another woman. Both women married to the same man!

Jacob, the son of Isaac, the son of Abraham, on the run from his brother Esau, was now looking for a wife. Rachel was beautiful and well favored. Her sister Leah was weak eyed. Jacob loved Rachel and agreed to work seven years for her. Laban, Rachel's father and Jacob's mother's brother, agreed with Jacob's plan.

Jacob worked seven years for the woman he loved. The years seemed to him to be a few days for the love he had for her. At the end of the seven-year period, Jacob asked Laban for the wife he had worked for. Laban gathered all the men of the place and gave a feast.

That evening of festivities, the wedding night, turned into a nightmare when Laban brought Leah

Looking for Love in the Wrong Place

to Jacob instead of Rachel. As was the custom of that country, the younger was not given in marriage before the older. As was the custom of the time, the veiled bride was taken into the bedchamber to her husband in silence and darkness. So Jacob, the trickster, was tricked and deceived by his father-in-law just as he had tricked his own brother Esau.

Jacob, with a bit of shrewd negotiations, had bought Esau's birthright for a bowl of lentils. Later Jacob, the youngest son, disguised and presented himself to his father, Isaac, as the firstborn and stole Esau's blessing (Genesis 25:29-34; 27:1-40). Likewise, Leah, the oldest daughter, by virtue of her father's deceit, was presented to Jacob as the younger, Rachel, and stole her blessing.

When Jacob awoke the next morning, Leah, not Rachel, was by his side. Laban told Jacob about the custom of not giving the younger before the older in marriage and that once he finished out the bridal week with Leah, then he could have Rachel. At the end of the week Jacob and Rachel consummated the marriage.

Two wives in one week. Two sisters married to the same man.

After that, Jacob had to work another seven years for Rachel. Jacob loved Rachel more than Leah (Genesis 29:30), so he worked.

Laban was successful in marrying off both of his daughters within a week of each other, but to the same man. The deceit of Laban not only affected Jacob, but also Leah and Rachel.

A Love Triangle

How did weak-eyed Leah feel about being practically forced upon Jacob because of the custom of the land and being the wife of the man who loved her sister? How did Leah feel toward her father, who appeared to use her to accomplish his purpose? How did beautiful Rachel feel, knowing that the man who loved her was sleeping with and married to her own sister? Think of the problems that lie ahead for this polygamous household. How did Rachel feel toward her father, who caused this schism, if there was one, between her and Jacob? How did Jacob feel toward Laban, who had tricked him, for the sake of custom, into becoming the husband of a woman he did not love or desire? How did Jacob feel toward Leah, who appeared to be a victim of circumstances? How could Jacob assure Rachel, his beloved?

What an explosion of emotions this whole event set off between husband and wife #1, husband and wife #2, sister and sister, father and both daughters, and also uncle and nephew (since Jacob was Laban's sister's son).

How does the sovereignty of God fit into this scenario? Was He paying attention? Did He allow all this to happen? Will God turn this mess into a message for them and for us?

Read Genesis 29:31-35 and make a list of everything you see about the Lord. Mark any form of *love* or *unloved* and list your findings.

Looking for Love in the Wrong Place

Genesis 29

³¹ Now the LORD saw that Leah was unloved, and He opened her womb, but Rachel was barren.

³² Leah conceived and bore a son and named him Reuben, for she said, "Because the LORD has seen my affliction; surely now my husband will love me."

³³ Then she conceived again and bore a son and said, "Because the LORD has heard that I am unloved, He has therefore given me this son also." So she named him Simeon.

³⁴ She conceived again and bore a son and said, "Now this time my husband will become attached to me, because I have borne him three sons." Therefore he was named Levi.

³⁵ And she conceived again and bore a son and said, "This time I will praise the LORD." Therefore she named him Judah. Then she stopped bearing.

About the Lord:

_____

_____

_____

About love:

_____

_____

_____

A Love Triangle

Read the text again. You will see from verses 31-35 above that Leah had four sons. Their names are listed below in order of their birth. Next to their names, write in the meaning of each name and what Leah says after each birth.

a. Reuben

_____

_____

_____

b. Simeon

_____

_____

_____

c. Levi

_____

_____

_____

d. Judah

_____

_____

_____

Looking for Love in the Wrong Place

From the text, answer the following questions. Does Leah know she is not loved? How does she seek to please her husband? What makes her think that God knows her problem? Does Leah acknowledge God? Is her focus on her sister, on her husband, on herself, or on God? Could she be looking for love in the wrong place? Record your findings.

_____

_____

_____

Mark any form of the word *love* and record what you learn about the love of God from the following verses. Wherever possible, answer in response to who, where, when, why, what, and how.

Jeremiah 31

[3] The LORD appeared to him from afar, saying, "I have loved you with an everlasting love; therefore I have drawn you with lovingkindness."

About love:

_____

_____

_____

A Love Triangle

John 14

²³ Jesus answered and said to him, "If anyone loves Me, he will keep My word; and My Father will love him, and We will come to him and make our abode with him."

About love:

_____

_____

_____

John 3

¹⁶ "For God so loved the world, that He gave His only begotten Son, that whoever believes in Him shall not perish, but have eternal life.

About love:

_____

_____

_____

Galatians 2

²⁰ I have been crucified with Christ; and it is no longer I who live, but Christ lives in me; and the life which I now live in the flesh I live by faith in the Son of God, who loved me and gave Himself up for me.

Looking for Love in the Wrong Place

About love:

_____

_____

_____

Is Rachel handling the situation any better than Leah? With a heart longing for children yet empty arms, Rachel cries out to her husband. Go back and read Genesis 29:31 and Genesis 30:1-8 below, noting her condition, her emotional state, and how she responds. Does she acknowledge God? Is Rachel's focus on her sister, on her husband, on her handmaid, on herself, or on God? Could she be looking to the love of a man to solve her problems? Is she looking for love in the wrong place? Answer each question and record the meaning of each name and what Rachel says after the birth of each of the handmaiden's (Bilhah) sons.

Genesis 30

¹ Now when Rachel saw that she bore Jacob no children, she became jealous of her sister; and she said to Jacob, "Give me children, or else I die."

² Then Jacob's anger burned against Rachel, and he said, "Am I in the place of God, who has withheld from you the fruit of the womb?"

³ She said, "Here is my maid Bilhah, go in to her that she may bear on my knees, that through her I too may have children."

A Love Triangle

⁴ So she gave him her maid Bilhah as a wife, and Jacob went in to her.
⁵ Bilhah conceived and bore Jacob a son.
⁶ Then Rachel said, "God has vindicated me, and has indeed heard my voice and has given me a son." Therefore she named him Dan.
⁷ Rachel's maid Bilhah conceived again and bore Jacob a second son.
⁸ So Rachel said, "With mighty wrestlings I have wrestled with my sister, and I have indeed prevailed." And she named him Naphtali.

a. Record Rachel's state:

_____

_____

_____

b. Dan (name meaning)

_____

_____

_____

c. Naphtali (name meaning)

_____

_____

_____

Looking for Love in the Wrong Place

Record what you learn about God in the following verses.

Psalm 34

¹⁸ The LORD is near to the brokenhearted and saves those who are crushed in spirit.

_____

_____

_____

Psalms 46

¹ God is our refuge and strength, a very present help in trouble.

_____

_____

_____

Psalm 91

¹ He who dwells in the shelter of the Most High will abide in the shadow of the Almighty.
² I will say to the LORD, "My refuge and my fortress, my God, in whom I trust!"
³ For it is He who delivers you from the snare of the trapper and from the deadly pestilence.
⁴ He will cover you with His pinions, and under His wings you may seek refuge; His faithfulness is a shield and bulwark.

A Love Triangle

Read Genesis 30:9-21. Just when it appears that Leah has settled down to praising God (the name of Leah's fourth son, Judah, means praise), she is back in the heat of the competition, using her handmaiden Zilpah against Rachel.

Genesis 30

9 When Leah saw that she had stopped bearing, she took her maid Zilpah and gave her to Jacob as a wife.

10 Leah's maid Zilpah bore Jacob a son.

11 Then Leah said, "How fortunate!" So she named him Gad.

12 Leah's maid Zilpah bore Jacob a second son.

13 Then Leah said, "Happy am I! For women will call me happy." So she named him Asher.

14 Now in the days of wheat harvest Reuben went and found mandrakes in the field, and brought them to his mother Leah. Then Rachel said to Leah, "Please give me some of your son's mandrakes."

15 But she said to her, "Is it a small matter for you to take my husband? And would you take my son's mandrakes also?" So Rachel said, "Therefore he may lie with you tonight in return for your son's mandrakes."

Looking for Love in the Wrong Place

¹⁶ When Jacob came in from the field in the evening, then Leah went out to meet him and said, "You must come in to me, for I have surely hired you with my son's mandrakes." So he lay with her that night.

¹⁷ God gave heed to Leah, and she conceived and bore Jacob a fifth son.

¹⁸ Then Leah said, "God has given me my wages because I gave my maid to my husband." So she named him Issachar.

¹⁹ Leah conceived again and bore a sixth son to Jacob.

²⁰ Then Leah said, "God has endowed me with a good gift; now my husband will dwell with me, because I have borne him six sons." So she named him Zebulun.

²¹ Afterward she bore a daughter and named her Dinah.

Does Leah acknowledge God? Is she living out what she knows God can do? Has she learned anything after all these years? Is she still looking for love in the wrong place? Is her focus on her sister, on her husband, on her handmaid, on herself, or on God? Record what Leah says after the birth of Zilpah's sons.

a. Gad

_____

_____

_____

A Love Triangle

b. Asher

_____

_____

_____

c. Describe Leah's attitude:

_____

_____

_____

Read Genesis 30:9-21 again. Notice the altercation over the mandrakes. Mandrakes are herbs considered to be aphrodisiac in nature and helpful in conception. The fruit, described as a love charm, was yellow, full of soft pulp and about the size of a large plum. It is said that the root, when eaten, would have the effect of relaxing the womb. Both Leah and Rachel wanted the mandrakes. How does Jacob fit into this picture? What does Leah say about her husband? (See verses 15, 16, and 20.) Does she acknowledge God? Is she living out what she knows God can do? Is her focus on Jacob, on her sister, on herself, or on God? Does she seem to be looking for love in the wrong place? Record what Leah says about her children after their births.

a. Issachar

_____

_____

_____

Looking for Love in the Wrong Place

b. Zebulun

_____

_____

_____

c. Dinah

_____

_____

_____

d. Describe Leah's state:

_____

_____

_____

Read Genesis 30:22-24; 35:16-21. At last, God remembers Rachel.

Genesis 30

²² Then God remembered Rachel, and God gave heed to her and opened her womb.
²³ So she conceived and bore a son and said, "God has taken away my reproach."
²⁴ She named him Joseph, saying, "May the LORD give me another son."

Does Rachel acknowledge God? Does she live out what she knows God can do? Does the birth of her son

A Love Triangle

change her in any way? Is she still looking to the love of a man to solve her problems? Is her focus on Jacob, on her sister, on herself, or on God? Record the name meaning and what is said after the birth of Joseph. Record your findings.

a. Describe Rachel's actions at this point.

_____

_____

_____

b. Joseph:

_____

_____

_____

After the birth of Joseph but before the birth of Benjamin, Jacob decided to return home. After much discussion, hard work, time, and careful planning, Jacob and his uncle Laban, the father of his wives, eventually worked out a solution. Jacob called his wives together and told them how Laban had manipulated his wages and also of the dream that directed him to return home. Amazingly, Leah and Rachel agreed to go with Jacob, essentially aligning themselves against their father, who wanted them to stay. Read Genesis 31:14-16 and underline their joint response.

Looking for Love in the Wrong Place

Genesis 31

¹⁴ Rachel and Leah said to him, "Do we still have any portion or inheritance in our father's house?

¹⁵ "Are we not reckoned by him as foreigners? For he has sold us, and has also entirely consumed our purchase price.

¹⁶ "Surely all the wealth which God has taken away from our father belongs to us and our children; now then, do whatever God has said to you."

Did you notice how the sisters had a united front as they provided input into Jacob's decision to return home? As they left Mesopotamia and traveled toward Canaan, Jacob had deep reservations about his brother Esau, who had threatened to kill him twenty years earlier. Read Genesis 33:1-3 and list the order of Jacob's wives and children as they see Esau coming toward them.

Genesis 33

¹ Then Jacob lifted his eyes and looked, and behold, Esau was coming, and four hundred men with him. So he divided the children among Leah and Rachel and the two maids.

² He put the maids and their children in front, and Leah and her children next, and Rachel and Joseph last.

³ But he himself passed on ahead of them and bowed down to the ground seven times, until he came near to his brother.

A Love Triangle

1st-

_____

_____

2nd-

_____

_____

3rd-

_____

_____

Jacob, still partial to Rachel, assigned Rachel and Joseph the safest place, last. At this point Rachel was pregnant. Jacob's fears turned out to be unfounded, for Esau embraced him, kissed him, and wept with him. (Read Genesis 35:16-21.) Again God remembered Rachel. Underline the events before and after the birth.

Genesis 35

16 Then they journeyed from Bethel; and when there was still some distance to go to Ephrath, Rachel began to give birth and she suffered severe labor.

17 When she was in severe labor the midwife said to her, "Do not fear, for now you have another son."

18 It came about as her soul was departing (for she died), that she named him Ben-oni; but his father called him Benjamin.

19 So Rachel died and was buried on the way to Ephrath (that is, Bethlehem).

20 Jacob set up a pillar over her grave; that is the pillar of Rachel's grave to this day.

Looking for Love in the Wrong Place

²¹ Then Israel journeyed on and pitched his tent beyond the tower of Eder.

Rachel named her second son Benoni, which means "son of my sorrow"; however, Jacob called him Benjamin, which means "son of my right hand." Jacob loved Rachel from the beginning (Genesis 29:18) until the very end, and Joseph was loved more than all of his other sons (Genesis 37:3). Interesting, isn't it?

Could Rachel and Leah have avoided all the emotional drama, the jealousy, the envy, the competition, the sustaining feelings of rejection, the plotting, the scheming, the struggles, the bitterness, the contention, and the strife for twenty years? Leah was unhappy because she was unloved by Jacob, although she had many sons. Rachel was loved, but she was unhappy because she was barren and could not bear children for Jacob. The one was looking for love in the wrong place; the other one was looking to the love of a man to solve her problems.

Even though Rachel and Leah both acknowledged God, did they really get love? Did they live out what they knew God could do? Write out your answers.

_____

_____

_____

God had a plan and a purpose for Rachel, Leah, and Jacob. Jacob's name was changed to Israel (Genesis 32:28). The sons borne by Rachel, Leah, and their

A Love Triangle

handmaids became the fathers of the twelve tribes of Israel. Although Jacob loved Rachel, God chose Leah to be the mother of the tribe through whom our Lord came: the tribe of Judah. Leah also bore Levi, the head of the priestly tribe. Leah is buried with Abraham, Sarah, Isaac, and Rebekah (Genesis 49).

On the other hand, God used Rachel, whom Jacob loved, to bear Joseph, who became the deliverer of Israel. God sent Joseph ahead of Israel into Egypt to preserve the nation. Rachel is buried on the road to Ephrath, which is Bethlehem. Her tomb became a landmark (noted in 1 Samuel 10:1-2, when Samuel anointed Saul). In Jeremiah 31:15, the prophet Jeremiah says the Lord speaks of Rachel weeping for her children and refuses to be comforted when all the children are carried away into exile in Babylon. This prophecy was quoted in Matthew 2:16-18, when Herod, seeking the Christ child, killed all the children in Bethlehem and the surrounding areas who were two years old and under.

Both Rachel and Leah are mentioned in Ruth 4:11, where Ruth is compared to Rachel and Leah, who built the house of Israel. The promise was given centuries ago to Abraham that all the families of the earth would be blessed. The covenant was cut with Abraham, passed to Isaac, and then the Jacob. The families of the world were blessed when God sent His Son to die for our sins. Now, that's love! Jesus laid down His life for us. That's love! And if you belong to Christ, you are Abraham's descendant, an heir according to the promise. Blessed!

Looking for love? Look to Jesus!

Looking for Love in the Wrong Place

Selah…Think about it.

1. Have you been in a situation similar to this one in one way or another? Have you ever felt used, rejected, unloved, discontented, looking for attention, acceptance, validation, and/or approval?

   _____

   _____

   _____

2. Have you allowed bitterness or resentment to hold you in bondage? Often the very thing that holds you in bondage is the thing you hold on to.

   _____

   _____

   _____

3. Are your expectations toward someone or something rather than God? Maybe you are sensitive and your feelings are easily hurt. Maybe you are unhappy with the circumstances in your life, whether in your family, on your job, in your church, or in your community. God has a plan and purpose for your life. Are you willing to settle for less than what God has planned

A Love Triangle

for you? Are you looking for love in the wrong place?

_____

_____

_____

4. Are you looking to the love of a man or a woman to solve your problems? Where is your focus—on yourself, on your circumstances, on someone else, or on God? Does focus really matter?

_____

_____

_____

5. How would you explain to someone how to look for love that will last and the impact that love can have in that person's life and in the lives of others?

_____

_____

_____

6. The first mention of love in the Bible concerns Jacob's grandfather, Abraham. Read Genesis 22 and record the event, the characters, and their relationships to one another. What basic prin-

Looking for Love in the Wrong Place

ciples of love do you see in this passage? Record your findings below:

_____

_____

_____

Read the following Scriptures and record what you learn from each.

Isaiah 26

³ You will keep him in perfect peace, whose mind is stayed on You, Because he trusts in You. (NKJV)

_____

_____

_____

Isaiah 41

¹⁰ Fear not, for I am with you; be not dismayed, for I am your God. I will strengthen you, yes, I will help you, I will uphold you with My righteous right hand. (NKJV)

_____

_____

_____

Are you convinced? Where is *your* focus? Have you sought answers in someone or something other than God and found despair, dissatisfaction, and broken

A Love Triangle

promises? Is there anyone who always keeps promises? Have you sought for love, a true unconditional love, from someone other than God and found disappointment or a broken heart?

If you are saved, you should have no trouble incorporating the verses we have studied. But did you get the message? Rachel and Leah didn't seem to. The idea is knowing God and what He can do, and totally lining up our lives with who He is and what He has promised to do in us.

Do you get it? *Really* get it? Are you acknowledging God and living out these Scriptures? Are you applying these Scriptures to your life day by day? Are you consistently living according to God's Word? To experience what God has planned for you and the purpose He established for your life before the foundation of the world, keep your focus on Him and daily live His Word. *Does God alone have your heart?*

Chapter 2

SHE LOVES ME?
POTIPHAR'S WIFE AND JOSEPH

The woman was prosperous, influential, and married to one of Egypt's top officials, the captain of Pharaoh's bodyguards. Joseph was a slave. A young man from Israel sold by his brothers (Jacob's sons) to his cousins (the Ishmaelites). They took him to Egypt and sold him to Potiphar, and he became his slave. The amazing thing is that the hand of the Lord was with him and he became a very successful man.

Joseph's behavior was obvious to Potiphar, who saw that God was with Joseph and how everything he did prospered in his hand. Joseph had such favor with Potiphar that he was made overseer of the house. Potiphar prospered and the Lord's blessing was on everything he owned, in the house and in the field, basically because Joseph was in the house (Gen. 39:1-6).

Looking for Love in the Wrong Place

Read Genesis 39:5-6. Record what you see about Joseph.

Genesis 39

⁵ It came about that from the time he made him overseer in his house and over all that he owned, the LORD blessed the Egyptian's house on account of Joseph; thus the LORD'S blessing was upon all that he owned, in the house and in the field.

⁶ So he left everything he owned in Joseph's charge; and with him there he did not concern himself with anything except the food which he ate. Now Joseph was handsome in form and appearance.

About Joseph:

_____

_____

_____

Read Genesis 29:17 and Genesis 30:27, and note how he takes after his mother, Rachel, and his father, Jacob.

Genesis 29

¹⁷ And Leah's eyes were weak, but Rachel was beautiful of form and face.

How was Joseph like his mother?

_____

_____

_____

She Loves Me?

Genesis 30

²⁷ But Laban said to him, "If now it pleases you, stay with me; I have divined that the LORD has blessed me on your account."

Laban is talking to Jacob here. How was Joseph like his father?

_____

_____

_____

Joseph, like his beautiful mother, was handsome in form and appearance, and like his father, possessed the favor of God and blessed others in his presence.

Potiphar's wife also noticed Joseph. Wonder if she picked up on the fact that much of the blessings of her household were because of him? She certainly did not miss that he was one handsome man. We find her looking for love (or perhaps more aptly described as lust) in the wrong place. Obviously she was a married woman, and everyone except her husband was off limits.

Read Genesis 39:7-12, noting all you see about Joseph and about Potiphar's wife. Underline the reasons Joseph gives for refusing her offer.

Genesis 39

7 It came about after these events that his master's wife looked with desire at Joseph, and she said, "Lie with me."

Looking for Love in the Wrong Place

⁸ But he refused and said to his master's wife, "Behold, with me here, my master does not concern himself with anything in the house, and he has put all that he owns in my charge.

⁹ "There is no one greater in this house than I, and he has withheld nothing from me except you, because you are his wife. How then could I do this great evil and sin against God?"

¹⁰ As she spoke to Joseph day after day, he did not listen to her to lie beside her or be with her.

¹¹ Now it happened one day that he went into the house to do his work, and none of the men of the household was there inside.

¹² She caught him by his garment, saying, "Lie with me!" And he left his garment in her hand and fled, and went outside.

Describe the character traits of Joseph and Potiphar's wife.

Mrs. P.:

_____

_____

_____

Joseph:

_____

_____

_____

She Loves Me?

It looks like Potiphar's wife had an eye problem as she "looked" at Joseph. Read the following passage underlining what Jesus says about looking.

Matthew 5

27 You have heard that it was said, "You shall not commit adultery";

28 but I say to you that everyone who looks at a woman with lust for her has already committed adultery with her in his heart.

Read Job 31:1 and underline Job's solution for "looking."

Job 31

1 I have made a covenant with my eyes; how then could I gaze at a virgin?

Read Job 31:6-12. Underline what Job says about his heart following his eyes and being enticed. Double underline what Job wants God to know.

Job 31

6 Let Him weigh me with accurate scales, and let God know my integrity.

7 If my step has turned from the way, or my heart followed my eyes, or if any spot has stuck to my hands,

8 Let me sow and another eat, and let my crops be uprooted.

Looking for Love in the Wrong Place

⁹ If my heart has been enticed by a woman, or I have lurked at my neighbor's doorway,
¹⁰ May my wife grind for another, and let others kneel down over her.
¹¹ For that would be a lustful crime; moreover, it would be an iniquity punishable by judges.
¹² For it would be fire that consumes to Abaddon, And would uproot all my increase.

Obviously Potiphar's wife was "looking" for something in the wrong place and she was not going to find it with Joseph. She completely underestimated Joseph's relationship to God and the high standards upheld by those who believed in Him. Mrs. P.'s attitude is much like what we see in the world today. It is no holds barred, whatever we want we take, totally driven by lust.

Read the following passages, underlining what the Bible says about sex outside of marriage. Record what will happen to those who do not repent and follow God's plan.

Exodus 20
¹⁴ You shall not commit adultery.

_____

_____

_____

She Loves Me?

Leviticus 20

¹⁰ If there is a man who commits adultery with another man's wife, one who commits adultery with his friend's wife, the adulterer and the adulteress shall surely be put to death.

_____

_____

_____

Ephesians 5

⁵ For this you know with certainty, that no immoral or impure person or covetous man, who is an idolater, has an inheritance in the kingdom of Christ and God.
⁶ Let no one deceive you with empty words, for because of these things the wrath of God comes upon the sons of disobedience.

_____

_____

_____

1 Thessalonians 4

³ For this is the will of God, your sanctification; that is, that you abstain from sexual immorality;
⁴ that each of you know how to possess his own vessel in sanctification and honor,

Looking for Love in the Wrong Place

⁵ not in lustful passion, like the Gentiles who do not know God;

___

___

___

Hebrews 13

⁴ Marriage is to be held in honor among all, and the marriage bed is to be undefiled; for fornicators and adulterers God will judge.

___

___

___

Revelation 21

⁸ But for the cowardly and unbelieving and abominable and murderers and immoral persons and sorcerers and idolaters and all liars, their part will be in the lake that burns with fire and brimstone, which is the second death.

___

___

___

There are numerous Scriptures on this subject. If you would like to look up a few more passages, check these

She Loves Me?

out: Proverbs 5:1-23; 6:20-35; 7:1-27. All were written primarily by Solomon, who had plenty of experience (with one thousand wives and concubines). Look at Deuteronomy 22:13-20 for additional information.

Mrs. P. was angry, but she was not one to be outdone. She knew Joseph was conscientious, but she had not counted on him being faithful to God and her husband, honest in all his dealings, and upright in every way. She had been rejected and perhaps humiliated by this young man, whose excuse was "How can I do this great evil and sin against God?" Not seeing this as an opportunity to seek God or to repent, she became furious and determined to take action against Joseph.

Read Genesis 39:13-20.

Genesis 39

^{13} When she saw that he had left his garment in her hand and had fled outside,

^{14} she called to the men of her household and said to them, "See, he has brought in a Hebrew to us to make sport of us; he came in to me to lie with me, and I screamed.

^{15} "When he heard that I raised my voice and screamed, he left his garment beside me and fled and went outside."

^{16} So she left his garment beside her until his master came home.

Looking for Love in the Wrong Place

¹⁷ Then she spoke to him with these words, "The Hebrew slave, whom you brought to us, came in to me to make sport of me;
¹⁸ "and as I raised my voice and screamed, he left his garment beside me and fled outside."
¹⁹ Now when his master heard the words of his wife, which she spoke to him, saying, "This is what your slave did to me," his anger burned.
²⁰ So Joseph's master took him and put him into the jail, the place where the king's prisoners were confined; and he was there in the jail.

This is not the first time Joseph's coat and a love relationship caused a problem for him. In Genesis 37:3, Jacob, Joseph's father, loved him more than all his sons and made him a coat of many colors. What appeared to be the beginning of Joseph's problems turned out to be a part of God's purpose for His people.

Out of jealousy, Joseph's brothers sought to destroy him. The rejected Mrs. Potiphar likewise plans her course. With Joseph's coat as evidence in her hand, she put the lie together. The advances she made toward Joseph and the desires she had for him became the basis of the lies against him. The young man, her would-be lover, who was so desirable before, has now become the villain, the "slave," the "Hebrew." The blame game begins.

Potiphar's wife may have been looking for love, companionship, attention, or just a "good time," but

She Loves Me?

she ran into more than simply a Hebrew slave. She had encountered a man of integrity who loved his God more than pleasure, more than obedience to the master's wife, and more than a job.

He reminded her that she was a married woman. Confronted with this fact, she seemed even more determined to have what she wanted at any cost. She pursued him daily, but to his credit, he refused to listen and always retreated from her advances.

Unfortunately she did not listen to Joseph and daily missed the kindness of God that could have led her to repentance. Looking for love in the wrong place, she missed the love of God that was continuously before her. Nothing Joseph said brought her to repentance or curbed her violent passion. She pressed, missed, pressed again and again, tried and lied. She not only accused Joseph, but also Potiphar, who had bought him.

Potiphar became angry. The crime worthy of death suddenly became a jail sentence. The sentence says a lot about Potiphar, who personally put Joseph in charge of other prisoners (Genesis 40:4). More than that, it speaks volumes about God. When God is the focus of your love and your actions, He will give you favor over and over again. Fact is, He surrounds the righteous with favor as with a shield (Ps. 5:12).

Read and underline God's promises in the following verses.

Looking for Love in the Wrong Place

Hebrews 13

⁵ Make sure that your character is free from the love of money, being content with what you have; for He Himself has said, "I will never desert you, nor will I ever forsake you,"
⁶ so that we confidently say, "The Lord is my helper, I will not be afraid. What will man do to me?"

God's promise is that He will never leave. As a result, our response is, "I will not be afraid. The Lord is my helper." With confidence we can say, "What can man do to me?"

Jeremiah 31

³ The LORD appeared to him from afar, saying, "I have loved you with an everlasting love; therefore I have drawn you with lovingkindness."

Lovingkindness is a covenant term, meaning "favor to close friends and family members." His promise is a love that is everlasting. No one can give you that kind of promise or that kind of love.

She Loves Me?

Selah…Think about it.

1. In spite of Joseph's situation (separation from family and homeland, and bondage in Egypt) as well as Potiphar's wife's accusation, what was God doing in Joseph's life? Is it possible for God to make you, and everyone around you, to prosper, even when you are in bondage? What, if anything, does attitude have to do with this?

   _____
   _____
   _____

2. Potiphar's wife was obviously lacking something in character and perhaps other areas. Was God doing anything in her life? Is there something you wish you had but you know it is forbidden? According to the Word of God, what are you to do?

   _____
   _____
   _____

3. List the principles that Joseph used (in Genesis 39) to resist temptation. Where do you suppose Joseph got his knowledge of right and wrong and his ability to reject sin?

Looking for Love in the Wrong Place

What would you say about Joseph's love for God based on the action he took?

_____

_____

_____

4. What did you learn about God in this study?

_____

_____

_____

5. What is God trying to teach you about your relationship with Him as a result of this study? List at least two things that God has taught you in this study, and spend time in prayer about the lessons learned.

_____

_____

_____

6. What would you say about your love for God based on the actions you take?

_____

_____

_____

She Loves Me?

7. How would you explain to someone how to look for love that will last and the impact that love can have on his or her life and the lives of others.

_____

_____

_____

Chapter 3

WHAT'S LOVE GOT TO DO WITH IT?
DAVID AND MICHAL

David was born during the time of transition from the judges to the kings. There was no king in Israel, and everyone was doing what was right in his own eyes. Israel, influenced by their neighbors, decided they wanted a king like all the surrounding nations had. Samuel, God's appointed prophet, intent on doing what was right in God's eyes, warned the people not to reject God for an earthly king. But the people would not listen, and Saul was chosen as king.

Saul, initially reluctant to be anointed as the king, soon came to trust more in himself than in God. He acted foolishly and did not keep the commands of God. God would command one thing, and rebellious Saul would go about doing things his way.

Looking for Love in the Wrong Place

Saul eventually admitted that he had transgressed the commands of God because he feared the people. With Saul's rejection of the Word of God, the kingdom was torn from his hands and given to his neighbor, who was a man after God's own heart. Samuel anointed David, a shepherd boy and the youngest of his brothers, as the king of Israel (1 Sam. 16).

Saul, the reigning king of Israel, terrorized by an evil spirit from God because of his disobedience, sought for and hired a musician to provide soothing music during the terrorizing attacks. As the music played, Saul would be refreshed and the evil spirit would depart from him. The musician was recognized as being very skillful, a mighty man of valor, prudent in speech, and a handsome man. It was said of him, "The Lord is with him." This musician and known worshipper of God was David, the forthcoming king. God placed David in a position in the palace to see firsthand the operation and workings of a king and his kingdom.

Saul had two daughters: Merab and Michal (MEE-kal, meaning "Who is like God?"). Michal, no doubt, had many opportunities to see the handsome, ruddy young shepherd boy as he played his harp for her father and befriended her brother Jonathan. David eventually became the nation's hero after the incredible victory over Goliath, the giant champion of the Philistines, who taunted the armies of the living God. The battle had been fought and the victory won, but Saul, the king, was not

What's Love Got to Do with It?

a happy man. Read 1 Samuel 18:6-9 to find out why. Underline your findings.

1 Samuel 18

6 It happened as they were coming, when David returned from killing the Philistine, that the women came out of all the cities of Israel, singing and dancing, to meet King Saul, with tambourines, with joy and with musical instruments.

7 The women sang as they played, and said, "Saul has slain his thousands, and David his ten thousands."

8 Then Saul became very angry, for this saying displeased him; and he said, "They have ascribed to David ten thousands, but to me they have ascribed thousands. Now what more can he have but the kingdom?"

9 Saul looked at David with suspicion from that day on.

Saul's anger had to be somewhat of a shock to David, for as long as he was playing the harp, "Saul loved him greatly, and he became his armor bearer" (1 Sam. 16:21). It did not seem to matter to Saul that the nation's enemy (Goliath, the Philistine) had been destroyed. Jealousy has a way of overshadowing the good.

Saul had promised a reward to the man who obtained victory over Goliath. The reward was Saul's daughter, great riches, and freedom for his father's house in Israel (1 Sam. 17:25).

Looking for Love in the Wrong Place

Read 1 Samuel 18:10-16. Mark the words *Lord, David,* and *Saul.* What is happening to the relationship between Saul and David?

1 Samuel 18

10 Now it came about on the next day that an evil spirit from God came mightily upon Saul, and he raved in the midst of the house, while David was playing the harp with his hand, as usual; and a spear was in Saul's hand.

11 Saul hurled the spear for he thought, "I will pin David to the wall." But David escaped from his presence twice.

12 Now Saul was afraid of David, for the LORD was with him but had departed from Saul.

13 Therefore Saul removed him from his presence and appointed him as his commander of a thousand; and he went out and came in before the people.

14 David was prospering in all his ways for the LORD was with him.

15 When Saul saw that he was prospering greatly, he dreaded him.

16 But all Israel and Judah loved David, and he went out and came in before them.

Read 1 Samuel 18:17-19, marking the words *David, Saul,* and *Lord.* Underline and record Saul's offer and David's response.

What's Love Got to Do with It?

¹⁷ Then Saul said to David, "Here is my older daughter Merab; I will give her to you as a wife, only be a valiant man for me and fight the LORD's battles." For Saul thought, "My hand shall not be against him, but let the hand of the Philistines be against him."
¹⁸ But David said to Saul, "Who am I, and what is my life or my father's family in Israel, that I should be the king's son-in-law?"
¹⁹ So it came about at the time when Merab, Saul's daughter, should have been given to David, that she was given to Adriel the Meholathite for a wife.

What was Saul's hidden agenda?

When David refused Saul's daughter Merab, Saul's plan against David was spoiled. It did not take long for a new scheme to emerge. Michal was waiting in the wings and it was her turn. It seemed that Saul, by hook or by crook, planned to destroy David.

Read 1 Samuel 18:20-29. Mark the names *David* and *Saul*. What is Saul's offer, and what is David's response? From this passage, why is Saul so angry with David?

1 Samuel 18

²⁰ Now Michal, Saul's daughter, loved David. When they told Saul, the thing was agreeable to him.
²¹ Saul thought, "I will give her to him that she may become a snare to him, and that the hand of

Looking for Love in the Wrong Place

the Philistines may be against him." Therefore Saul said to David, "For a second time you may be my son-in-law today."

²² Then Saul commanded his servants, "Speak to David secretly, saying, 'Behold, the king delights in you, and all his servants love you; now therefore, become the king's son-in-law.'"

²³ So Saul's servants spoke these words to David. But David said, "Is it trivial in your sight to become the king's son-in-law, since I am a poor man and lightly esteemed?"

²⁴ The servants of Saul reported to him according to these words which David spoke.

²⁵ Saul then said, "Thus you shall say to David, 'The king does not desire any dowry except a hundred foreskins of the Philistines, to take vengeance on the king's enemies.'" Now Saul planned to make David fall by the hand of the Philistines.

²⁶ When his servants told David these words, it pleased David to become the king's son-in-law. Before the days had expired

²⁷ David rose up and went, he and his men, and struck down two hundred men among the Philistines. Then David brought their foreskins, and they gave them in full number to the king, that he might become the king's son-in-law. So Saul gave him Michal his daughter for a wife.

²⁸ When Saul saw and knew that the LORD was with David, and that Michal, Saul's daughter, loved him,

What's Love Got to Do with It?

²⁹ then Saul was even more afraid of David. Thus Saul was David's enemy continually.

_____

_____

_____

From the verses above and the definition below for the word *snare* in 1 Samuel 18:21, make a list of Saul's plans for David. Also compare 1 Samuel 16:21 with 1 Samuel 18:12, 29. How would you describe Saul and David's relationship?

Word Study

The Hebrew word for *snare* is *mowqesh* (mo-kashe′) or *moqesh* (mo-kashe). It means "a noose (for catching animals) (literally or figuratively): by implication, a hook (for the nose):–be ensnared, trap."

Michal loved David, and Saul knew it. Saul planned to use Michal's love for his own purposes to trap David. But his plan did not work. Saul had not thought David would return alive. He was not only angry, he was also afraid—a dangerous and deadly combination.

He revealed his plan to kill David to all his servants and to his son Jonathan. He did not expect his son to defend David. But Jonathan reminded his father how he had rejoiced when David killed Goliath and brought

Looking for Love in the Wrong Place

deliverance to the nation Israel. He challenged Saul's plan to shed the innocent blood of David without cause. Saul listened to Jonathan and vowed not to kill David. Notwithstanding Saul's vow, Jonathan warned David to be on guard.

David and Michal were married, but the wars continued. David fought the Philistines with a great slaughter and defeated them. Back in the palace, David continued to play the harp whenever an evil spirit came upon Saul. Once again Saul hurled a spear at David and missed as he escaped into the night.

Saul sent men to watch David's house and to kill him the next morning. Read Psalm 59:1; 16-17 to grasp David's view of what was happening in his life. Underline David's request and his attitude.

Psalm 59

¹ <<For the choir director; set to Al-tashheth. A Mikhtam of David, when Saul sent men and they watched the house in order to kill him.>> Deliver me from my enemies, O my God; Set me securely on high away from those who rise up against me.

¹⁶ But as for me, I shall sing of Your strength; yes, I shall joyfully sing of Your lovingkindness in the morning, for You have been my stronghold And a refuge in the day of my distress.

¹⁷ O my strength, I will sing praises to You; for God is my stronghold, the God who shows me lovingkindness.

What's Love Got to Do with It?

The markings << and >> in verse 1 are brackets that enclose the setting, description, and title information about the Psalm. The actual Psalm begins with "Deliver me from my enemies…" It is clear that David's theme song is God's lovingkindness, and the basis of his strength is God in the midst of trouble. The favor and love David is looking for is from God and God alone.

Read the entire Psalm in your Bible and underline all you see about God. What do you learn from David's attitude in the midst of a crisis? What do you learn about God?

_____

_____

_____

Read 1 Samuel 19:11-17. Mark *David, Michal,* and *Saul.* Describe Michal's role in David's escape.

1 Samuel 19

¹¹ Then Saul sent messengers to David's house to watch him, in order to put him to death in the morning. But Michal, David's wife, told him, saying, "If you do not save your life tonight, tomorrow you will be put to death."
¹² So Michal let David down through a window, and he went out and fled and escaped.

Looking for Love in the Wrong Place

¹³ Michal took the household idol and laid it on the bed, and put a quilt of goats' hair at its head, and covered it with clothes.

¹⁴ When Saul sent messengers to take David, she said, "He is sick."

¹⁵ Then Saul sent messengers to see David, saying, "Bring him up to me on his bed, that I may put him to death."

¹⁶ When the messengers entered, behold, the household idol was on the bed with the quilt of goats' hair at its head.

¹⁷ So Saul said to Michal, "Why have you deceived me like this and let my enemy go, so that he has escaped?" And Michal said to Saul, "He said to me, 'Let me go! Why should I put you to death?'"

Saul had not counted on Michal's love for David to exceed her love and loyalty for her own father. She knew exactly what to do, even to placing the idol in the bed. (What's that man-sized idol doing in the palace?) She knew the words to say so her father would believe the lie and not put her to death.

David escaped with a contract on his life, and the wife who risked her life was left behind—a separation that was to last for years.

Time marched on, Saul was killed, David became the reigning king of Israel, and there was a long war between the house of David and the house of Saul. But, what about Michal? What about their marriage? Read

What's Love Got to Do with It?

1 Samuel 25:44. Mark *David* and *Michal* and record your findings.

1 Samuel 25

⁴⁴ Now Saul had given Michal his daughter, David's wife, to Palti the son of Laish, who was from Gallim.

These were polygamous times, but it was unusual that a woman would have more than one husband. We more often see that the man has more than one wife. Saul made the arrangements. And did you notice—Michal is still called David's wife.

Things have changed for David as well. By this time David had six sons by six different women and was the reigning king over Judah. Ishbosheth, Saul's son, had been made king over Israel (1 Sam. 2:8-9). Abner, Saul's uncle and the captain of Israel's army, became so angry with Ishbosheth that he sought to make a covenant with David so he could take over the kingdom of the entire nation. David agreed, but demanded one thing. Read 1 Samuel 3:12-16 to find out what David wanted. Mark *David* and *Michal*.

2 Samuel 3

¹² Then Abner sent messengers to David in his place, saying, "Whose is the land? Make your covenant with me, and behold, my hand shall be with you to bring all Israel over to you."

Looking for Love in the Wrong Place

¹³ He said, "Good! I will make a covenant with you, but I demand one thing of you, namely, you shall not see my face unless you first bring Michal, Saul's daughter, when you come to see me."

¹⁴ So David sent messengers to Ish-bosheth, Saul's son, saying, "Give me my wife Michal, to whom I was betrothed for a hundred foreskins of the Philistines."

¹⁵ Ish-bosheth sent and took her from her husband, from Paltiel the son of Laish.

¹⁶ But her husband went with her, weeping as he went, and followed her as far as Bahurim. Then Abner said to him, "Go, return." So he returned.

What is this all about? Love, politics, revenge, or what? Princess Michal, even from the beginning, did not seem to have much to say about who would be her husband—not to her father the king, her brother the king, or her husband the king.

Paltiel, Michal's current husband, had a difficult time letting go, weeping all the way. Interesting that she was not weeping! So Michal was returned to David, but David was fighting wars and conquering kingdoms. David became greater and greater, and he realized that the Lord had established him as king over Israel, and that God had exalted his kingdom for the sake of His people Israel (2 Sam. 5:12).

Back at the palace things had changed considerably, as Michal found out when she was added to David's

What's Love Got to Do with It?

growing harem of wives and concubines. It was not at all like the old days when she was the only wife and his attention was focused on her. And the children! Every wife and concubine had at least one child, except Michal.

More battles were fought and the Philistines were defeated. David made plans to finally bring the Ark of the Covenant back to Jerusalem the right way, the way God outlined in His Word. The ark had been lodged in Kiriath-jearim after its return out of captivity among the Philistines (1 Sam. 7:1-2). King Saul reigned over Israel for forty-two years with barely a mention of the ark. Saul had no regard for the ark and it was neglected.

David's plan to bring the ark into Jerusalem came with a high time of celebrating and worshipping, and for good reason. The Ark of the Covenant was a vivid reminder of Israel's covenant relationship with God. Inside was a jar of manna, the tables of the covenant, and Aaron's budded rod (Heb. 9:4). Over the mercy seat of the ark, between the cherubim, was where the Shekinah glory of God would abide, and where God promised to meet His people (Ex. 25:21-22).

Three months had passed since the life of Uzza had been snuffed out when they tried to bring the ark back on a cart. The Levites knew better this time, and so did David. The ark was to be carried on poles by the priests from the tribe of Levi. The Levites led the celebration, saying to the people, "Let the heart of those who seek the Lord be glad." (1 Chronicles 16:10).

Looking for Love in the Wrong Place

The Ark of the Covenant was being returned to the city and everyone was excited—well, almost everyone. Read 2 Samuel 6:12-16. Mark *David* and *Michal*. Why was Michal so resentful?

Underline the events of the chapter. Circle references to the ark.

2 Samuel 6

¹² Now it was told King David, saying, "The LORD has blessed the house of Obed-edom and all that belongs to him, on account of the ark of God." David went and brought up the ark of God from the house of Obed-edom into the city of David with gladness.

¹³ And so it was, that when the bearers of the ark of the LORD had gone six paces, he sacrificed an ox and a fatling.

¹⁴ And David was dancing before the LORD with all his might, and David was wearing a linen ephod.

¹⁵ So David and all the house of Israel were bringing up the ark of the LORD with shouting and the sound of the trumpet.

¹⁶ Then it happened as the ark of the LORD came into the city of David that Michal the daughter of Saul looked out of the window and saw King David leaping and dancing before the LORD; and she despised him in her heart.

What's Love Got to Do with It?

Why was Michal angry?

_____

_____

_____

Word Study

The Hebrew word for *despise* is *bazah* (baw-zaw'), meaning "to disesteem:–despise, disdain, contemptible, think to scorn; a vile person."

Despised him? What happened to the love of a young, courageous girl who risked her life for David, favoring him over her father?

Despised in verse 16 is also used to describe Esau when he "despised" his birthright, trading it for a bowl of lentils (Gen. 25:34), for which he was called godless and immoral (Heb. 12:16).

Michal had deep contempt for her husband, the king, for the way he was behaving. David, the man after God's own heart, was worshipping God from his heart, and his wife had a problem with him. And she let him know it! Out of her mouth came the issue of her heart.

This princess grew up in a palace, and she was the daughter of a king and the sister of a king. This woman's father had rejected the word of God and God had rejected him from being king. This woman had kept a

Looking for Love in the Wrong Place

man-sized idol in the house. Michal had experienced some tragic situations, was raised in a dysfunctional family, had been tossed from husband to husband, was a very unhappy woman, and could not or would not celebrate God. She was obviously missing something in her relationship with God and did not know or care about real worship. This often happens when someone is on the outside looking in, or in this case, on the inside looking out.

Read 2 Samuel 6:17-19, underlining what David does "before the Lord" and for the people.

2 Samuel 6

¹⁷ So they brought in the ark of the LORD and set it in its place inside the tent which David had pitched for it; and David offered burnt offerings and peace offerings before the LORD.

¹⁸ When David had finished offering the burnt offering and the peace offering, he blessed the people in the name of the LORD of hosts.

¹⁹ Further, he distributed to all the people, to all the multitude of Israel, both to men and women, a cake of bread and one of dates and one of raisins to each one. Then all the people departed each to his house.

What a celebration! David was excited, making offerings to the Lord and blessing all the people. The entire nation celebrated God. The Levites were appointed to

What's Love Got to Do with It?

sing hymns to God with instruments of music—harps and loud cymbals—and with shouts of joy. The people of the nation joined in singing the psalms and dancing before the Lord. The air was electric with thanks, praise, and worship, all directed toward the God of Israel.

With obvious satisfaction and focused on pleasing God, but unaware of Michal's disposition, David returned to bless his household. Read 2 Samuel 6:20 and underline the words describing his reception from Michal.

2 Samuel 6

20 But when David returned to bless his household, Michal the daughter of Saul came out to meet David and said, "How the king of Israel distinguished himself today! He uncovered himself today in the eyes of his servants' maids as one of the foolish ones shamelessly uncovers himself!"

Word Study

The Hebrew word for *uncovers* and *shamelessly* is the same: *galah* (gaw-law'), meaning "to denude (especially in a disgraceful sense); by implication, to exile (captives being usually stripped); figuratively, to reveal: advertise, appear, bring, (carry, lead, go) captive (into captivity), depart, disclose, discover, exile, be gone, open, plainly, publish, remove, reveal, shamelessly, shew, surely, tell, uncover."

Looking for Love in the Wrong Place

David had laid aside his royal robes and donned a linen ephod. Michal seemed to be concerned about how he looked to others. He had not distinguished himself as a king. He was not naked, but as far as she was concerned his behavior was shameless, foolish, and despicable.

David's response to Michal was unforgettable. Read 2 Samuel 6:21-23 and underline each point.

2 Samuel 6

21 So David said to Michal, "It was before the LORD, who chose me above your father and above all his house, to appoint me ruler over the people of the LORD, over Israel; therefore I will celebrate before the LORD.

22 "I will be more lightly esteemed than this and will be humble in my own eyes, but with the maids of whom you have spoken, with them I will be distinguished."

23 Michal the daughter of Saul had no child to the day of her death.

David pointed out his reasons for celebrating God: (A) He, not Saul, was God's choice for king. God had chosen David, and he was a man after God's own heart; Saul was not. This alone was enough to celebrate before God. (B) He would be more highly esteemed and would remain humble. God knew his heart. And the people understood his relationship with God, the importance of bringing the ark into the city, and all that it represented to the nation of Israel. He would be highly respected

What's Love Got to Do with It?

and would remain humble. (C) Even with the maids, he would be distinguished.

Michal did not get the point of David's display of worship, but the maids seemed to understand. David was not ashamed of worshipping God in this manner.

Michal's father, Saul, was prideful and arrogant, doing things his own way, completely rebellious and insubordinate to God. Saul had disregarded the ark of God and had rejected God and His word, and God had rejected Saul.

Was Michal caught in the trap of rebellion, too, also rejecting God, His word and His love? Michal's complaint to David seemed to mirror her own relationship with God. It was not about dancing; it was about a life dedicated to God and loving Him with a whole heart. Read Micah 6:6-8 and underline what the Lord requires.

Micah 6

⁶ With what shall I come before the LORD, and bow myself before the High God? Shall I come before Him with burnt offerings, with calves a year old?

⁷ Will the LORD be pleased with thousands of rams, Ten thousand rivers of oil? Shall I give my firstborn for my transgression, the fruit of my body for the sin of my soul?

⁸ He has shown you, O man, what is good; and what does the LORD require of you but to do justly, to love mercy, and to walk humbly with your God? (NKJV)

Looking for Love in the Wrong Place

Selah…Think about it.

1. It is clear from Scripture that Michal loved David, but did David love Michal? Could this have affected her relationship to God? What recourses are available to those who are not shown sufficient love by others? Provide Scripture to support your answer.

   _____

   _____

   _____

2. How do you see worship in 2 Samuel 6? In this passage, when does worship start and when does it end? What do you know about Michal's relationship with God? Don't forget the household idol.

   _____

   _____

   _____

3. What do you know about David's relationship with God? Include your findings from all the passages we have studied in this lesson.

   _____

   _____

   _____

What's Love Got to Do with It?

4. Read 1 Chronicles 16:1-36. How did the people respond in worship? Do you see freedom in their worship? Would you ever dance like David danced? How do you celebrate the Lord?

   _____

   _____

   _____

5. What does love have to do with our worship of God?

   _____

   _____

   _____

6. After David was delivered from the hands of his enemies and from Saul, he spoke the words of the song in 2 Samuel 22. Read the song and describe David's relationship with the Lord. What about you? Are you confident with who you are in God? Do you know in whom you believe, and are you convinced of God's love for you?

   _____

   _____

   _____

Looking for Love in the Wrong Place

David and Abigail

The events surrounding the meeting of David and Abigail occurred when David, the anointed but not ruling king, was hiding from Saul, the ruling king in the wilderness of Paran. David, on the run from Saul, had gathered around him about six hundred followers, who constituted a bodyguard and voluntarily protected the flocks of many herdsmen from prowling thieves.

In the sheep-and-goat country west of the Dead Sea, not far from where David was, lay the town of Moan. Nearby, standing in mountainous country, was the larger town of Carmel. One of the richest men in this area was Nabal, Abigail's husband. Read 1 Samuel 25:1-8 and record all you learn about Nabal and Abigail.

1 Samuel 25

[1] Then Samuel died; and all Israel gathered together and mourned for him, and buried him at his house in Ramah. And David arose and went down to the wilderness of Paran.

[2] Now there was a man in Maon whose business was in Carmel; and the man was very rich, and he had three thousand sheep and a thousand goats. And it came about while he was shearing his sheep in Carmel

[3] (now the man's name was Nabal, and his wife's name was Abigail. And the woman was intelligent and beautiful in appearance, but the man was harsh and evil in his dealings, and he was a Calebite),

What's Love Got to Do with It?

⁴ that David heard in the wilderness that Nabal was shearing his sheep.

⁵ So David sent ten young men; and David said to the young men, "Go up to Carmel, visit Nabal and greet him in my name;

⁶ and thus you shall say, "Have a long life, peace be to you, and peace be to your house, and peace be to all that you have.

⁷ "Now I have heard that you have shearers; now your shepherds have been with us and we have not insulted them, nor have they missed anything all the days they were in Carmel.

⁸ "Ask your young men and they will tell you. Therefore let my young men find favor in your eyes, for we have come on a festive day. Please give whatever you find at hand to your servants and to your son David.'"

Nabal: Abigail:

Abigail was beautiful, Nabal was rich, and on the surface they may have looked like the couple of the year. But *Abigail* and *Nabal* were not the most dynamic match of the century. She was an intelligent and wise woman, but he was harsh, evil in his dealings, and such a worthless man that no one could speak to him. Everyone knew he was a foolish man.

Looking for Love in the Wrong Place

What was David's request to Nabal in verses 1-8 above?

Read 1 Samuel 25:9-13. Underline Nabal's response and David's solution to this apparent problem.

1 Samuel 25

⁹ When David's young men came, they spoke to Nabal according to all these words in David's name; then they waited.

¹⁰ But Nabal answered David's servants and said, "Who is David? And who is the son of Jesse? There are many servants today who are each breaking away from his master.

¹¹ "Shall I then take my bread and my water and my meat that I have slaughtered for my shearers, and give it to men whose origin I do not know?"

¹² So David's young men retraced their way and went back; and they came and told him according to all these words.

¹³ David said to his men, "Each of you gird on his sword." So each man girded on his sword. And David also girded on his sword, and about four hundred men went up behind David while two hundred stayed with the baggage.

How does Nabal's response reflect his character?

_____

_____

_____

What's Love Got to Do with It?

Nabal is of the house of Caleb and of the tribe of Judah. What impact does Nabal's family heritage have on his character, since both men are of the tribe of Judah? Should their common heritage make a difference in how he treated David and his men?

Read 1 Samuel 25:14-20 and mark *Abigail* and *Nabal*. Also underline the reason the men are talking to Abigail and not to Nabal.

1 Samuel 25

14 But one of the young men told Abigail, Nabal's wife, saying, "Behold, David sent messengers from the wilderness to greet our master, and he scorned them.

15 "Yet the men were very good to us, and we were not insulted, nor did we miss anything as long as we went about with them, while we were in the fields.

16 "They were a wall to us both by night and by day, all the time we were with them tending the sheep.

17 "Now therefore, know and consider what you should do, for evil is plotted against our master and against all his household; and he is such a worthless man that no one can speak to him."

18 Then Abigail hurried and took two hundred loaves of bread and two jugs of wine and five sheep already prepared and five measures of roasted grain and a hundred clusters of raisins and two hundred cakes of figs, and loaded them on donkeys.

19 She said to her young men, "Go on before me; behold, I am coming after you." But she did not tell her husband Nabal.

Looking for Love in the Wrong Place

²⁰ It came about as she was riding on her donkey and coming down by the hidden part of the mountain, that behold, David and his men were coming down toward her; so she met them.

It is sheep-shearing time at the home of Nabal and Abigail. On such festive occasions, many guests would gather to eat, drink, and celebrate. It seemed natural that David and his men, who had helped Nabal's shepherds, would be welcome during this feasting time, but Nabal refused.

A woman of understanding, Abigail prepared to meet the king, gathering supplies to fulfill David's request. From the passage above answer, what she did, why she did it, and how she did it. Also list Abigail's weaknesses and strengths.

What?

_____

_____

_____

Why?

_____

_____

_____

What's Love Got to Do with It?

How?

_____

_____

_____

Strengths   Weaknesses

Abigail does not waste time weeping over the situation, and she does not discuss David's anger with her already angry, foolish husband. She simply sets about, with God, to handle the problem. Read 1 Samuel 25:21-22, then go back and reread 1 Samuel 25:13 to get a glimpse of David's attitude.

> **1 Samuel 25**
> 21 Now David had said, "Surely in vain I have guarded all that this man has in the wilderness, so that nothing was missed of all that belonged to him; and he has returned me evil for good.
> 22 "May God do so to the enemies of David, and more also, if by morning I leave as much as one male of any who belong to him."

Analyze David's reaction in 1 Samuel 25:13; 21-22. Was this a correct response for this soon to be "ruling king"? Why or why not? Can you support your answer with Scripture?

Looking for Love in the Wrong Place

Read 1 Samuel 25:23-31. Mark *Abigail* and any pronouns pertaining to her.

1 Samuel 25

23 When Abigail saw David, she hurried and dismounted from her donkey, and fell on her face before David and bowed herself to the ground.

24 She fell at his feet and said, "On me alone, my lord, be the blame. And please let your maidservant speak to you, and listen to the words of your maidservant.

25 "Please do not let my lord pay attention to this worthless man, Nabal, for as his name is, so is he. Nabal is his name and folly is with him; but I your maidservant did not see the young men of my lord whom you sent.

26 "Now therefore, my lord, as the LORD lives, and as your soul lives, since the LORD has restrained you from shedding blood, and from avenging yourself by your own hand, now then let your enemies and those who seek evil against my lord, be as Nabal.

27 "Now let this gift which your maidservant has brought to my lord be given to the young men who accompany my lord.

28 "Please forgive the transgression of your maidservant; for the LORD will certainly make for my lord an enduring house, because my lord is fighting the

What's Love Got to Do with It?

battles of the LORD, and evil will not be found in you all your days.

[29] "Should anyone rise up to pursue you and to seek your life, then the life of my lord shall be bound in the bundle of the living with the LORD your God; but the lives of your enemies He will sling out as from the hollow of a sling.

[30] "And when the LORD does for my lord according to all the good that He has spoken concerning you, and appoints you ruler over Israel,

[31] this will not cause grief or a troubled heart to my lord, both by having shed blood without cause and by my lord having avenged himself. When the LORD deals well with my lord, then remember your maidservant."

How would you describe Abigail's relationship to God? Realizing that she is between two angry men, how would you describe her knowledge of men and her tolerance for their bad behavior? Evaluate her petition to David, her encouragement to him, and her prediction and prophecy of future events.

Abigail and God:

_____

_____

_____

Looking for Love in the Wrong Place

Knowledge of men and tolerance for bad behavior:

_____

_____

_____

Abigail's petition to David:

_____

_____

_____

Her encouragement and prophecy:

_____

_____

_____

With all due respect to her husband and to David, she nailed the issue! With God guiding every action and word, Abigail risked her life and saved the lives in her household, and David's life was forever changed. Regardless of our circumstances, God has given us the ability to rise above them, to live and respond in a godly manner in every area of our lives. Read 1 Samuel 25:32-35 and underline David's response to Abigail's request.

1 Samuel 25

[32] Then David said to Abigail, "Blessed be the LORD God of Israel, who sent you this day to meet me,

What's Love Got to Do with It?

³³ and blessed be your discernment, and blessed be you, who have kept me this day from bloodshed and from avenging myself by my own hand.
³⁴ "Nevertheless, as the LORD God of Israel lives, who has restrained me from harming you, unless you had come quickly to meet me, surely there would not have been left to Nabal until the morning light as much as one male."
³⁵ So David received from her hand what she had brought him and said to her, "Go up to your house in peace. See, I have listened to you and granted your request."

The Word of God brings humility, confession, and repentance, especially when you have a heart after God. As the music of David's harp calmed King Saul during his tirades, the Word of God calmed David's spirit so that he recognized God working in Abigail. He listened to her and honored her request.

Would to God that we would respond in haste when God calls us to a task and that we would have ears to hear when God uses others to speak His Word to us. Think of the lives that could be saved, the wrong choices that could be averted, the blessings that could be attained, and above all, how God could be glorified!

Read 1 Samuel 25:36-38 and mark *Nabal, Abigail,* and *Lord.*

Looking for Love in the Wrong Place

1 Samuel 25

36 Then Abigail came to Nabal, and behold, he was holding a feast in his house, like the feast of a king. And Nabal's heart was merry within him, for he was very drunk; so she did not tell him anything at all until the morning light.

37 But in the morning, when the wine had gone out of Nabal, his wife told him these things, and his heart died within him so that he became as a stone.

38 About ten days later, the LORD struck Nabal and he died.

The feast was in full swing. It appears that Nabal did not realize that Abigail had been gone, nor that he'd had a near-death experience. Abigail decided not to tell him what happened until he was sober.

We can see from this story how serious God is about sin and about protecting His people. He is against evil and wickedness, but He will avenge His own people. Read 1 Samuel 25:39-44 and mark *David, Nabal, Abigail,* and *Lord.* Underline David's proposal and Abigail's response.

1 Samuel 25:39-44

39 When David heard that Nabal was dead, he said, "Blessed be the LORD, who has pleaded the cause of my reproach from the hand of Nabal and has kept back His servant from evil. The LORD has also

What's Love Got to Do with It?

returned the evildoing of Nabal on his own head." Then David sent a proposal to Abigail, to take her as his wife.

⁴⁰ When the servants of David came to Abigail at Carmel, they spoke to her, saying, "David has sent us to you to take you as his wife."

⁴¹ She arose and bowed with her face to the ground and said, "Behold, your maidservant is a maid to wash the feet of my lord's servants."

⁴² Then Abigail quickly arose, and rode on a donkey, with her five maidens who attended her; and she followed the messengers of David and became his wife.

⁴³ David had also taken Ahinoam of Jezreel, and they both became his wives.

⁴⁴ Now Saul had given Michal his daughter, David's wife, to Palti the son of Laish, who was from Gallim.

Abigail humbly accepted David's proposal, but I notice that she "quickly arose" to the occasion and became his wife. At this point David does not even have a house; he is on the run from Saul. Abigail brought with her a rich estate as well as her beauty, intellect, and understanding. An excellent wife, who can find? For her worth is far above jewels. The heart of her husband trusts in her, And he will have no lack of gain. (Prov. 31:10-11).

Looking for Love in the Wrong Place

Selah…Think about it.

1. Was Abigail out of order for not telling her husband right away that evil was plotted against him and the entire household? Read Proverbs 14:7; 17:27-28; 29:11. How does Ephesians 5:22 fit into this scenario?

   _____

   _____

   _____

2. Abigail obviously gained the respect and faithfulness of her household. She also acted in haste, without pausing to complain or to rehearse her pain. She knows how to live with a husband such as hers. What was her secret? What steps would you take to build such character and integrity in your life?

   _____

   _____

   _____

3. How do you suppose Abigail knew of the future events in David's life? Compare 1 Samuel 25:28 with 2 Samuel 7:11, 16.

   _____

   _____

   _____

What's Love Got to Do with It?

4. Both Nabal and David made bad choices. How do you react when someone in authority makes a bad choice that will affect you? Would you be as efficient and wise as Abigail?

   _____

   _____

   _____

5. Abigail goes down in history as a great woman of wisdom. What can we learn from her? What do you learn about wisdom from the following verses?

Psalm 119:169

_____

_____

_____

Proverbs 2:6; 3:13-24

_____

_____

_____

Ecclesiastes 7:19

_____

_____

_____

Looking for Love in the Wrong Place

Hosea 14:9

_____

_____

_____

Colossians 1:9-11

_____

_____

_____

James 1:5; 3:17

_____

_____

_____

6. What does love have to do with the relationship of David and Abigail?

_____

_____

_____

What's Love Got to Do with It?

David and Bathsheba

It was springtime in Israel, with trees budding, flowers blooming, and the air permeated with all the mixed fragrances. Springtime also meant wartime; the latter rains had passed and the ground was firm for marching soldiers.

Having reigned over Israel for about twelve years at this point, David, quite the warrior, continued to excel at fighting the Lord's battles, and the Lord helped him wherever he went.

After the battle with the Syrians, the Ammonites declared war against Israel. Kings usually went to war with their troops, but this time David decided to stay in Jerusalem, sending Joab and his army to the battlefield.

David had a growing quiver of children and at least seven wives and concubines, including Michal and the wise and beautiful Abigail. One evening David rose from his bed and took a walk on his roof. He saw a beautiful woman bathing nearby.

Underline David's actions in this passage.

2 Samuel 11

2 Now when evening came David arose from his bed and walked around on the roof of the king's house, and from the roof he saw a woman bathing; and the woman was very beautiful in appearance.

Looking for Love in the Wrong Place

> ³ So David sent and inquired about the woman. And one said, "Is this not Bathsheba, the daughter of Eliam, the wife of Uriah the Hittite?"
> ⁴ David sent messengers and took her, and when she came to him, he lay with her; and when she had purified herself from her uncleanness, she returned to her house.

Not satisfied with a look, David sent and inquired about her. He was told that the woman, Bathsheba, was married to Uriah, the Hittite, and was the daughter of Eliam, both of whom were honored among the thirty mighty men of David. She was also the granddaughter of Ahithophel, David's counselor.

Although well equipped with a palace full of his own wives, David sent for the wife of one of his mighty men and lay with her. What happened to this king, who'd been anointed and appointed by God, a magnificent warrior who had slain his ten thousands, and above all a man after God's own heart? Read the following Scriptures to see what could have caused the problem. Record your findings under each passage.

James 1

> ¹⁴ But each one is tempted when he is carried away and enticed by his own lust.
> ¹⁵ Then when lust has conceived, it gives birth to sin; and when sin is accomplished, it brings forth death.

What's Love Got to Do with It?

How does this passage describe what happened to David? Did he have a choice?

_____

_____

_____

1 Corinthians 10

13 No temptation has overtaken you but such as is common to man; and God is faithful, who will not allow you to be tempted beyond what you are able, but with the temptation will provide the way of escape also, so that you will be able to endure it.

How does this passage describe what happened to David? Did he have a choice?

_____

_____

_____

Galatians 5

16 But I say, walk by the Spirit, and you will not carry out the desire of the flesh.
17 For the flesh sets its desire against the Spirit, and the Spirit against the flesh; for these are in opposition to one another, so that you may not do the things that you please.

Looking for Love in the Wrong Place

How does this passage describe what happened to David? Did he have a choice?

_____

_____

_____

Read Genesis 3:6-7, comparing Eve's actions with those of David. Underline the similarities you see.

Genesis 3

6 When the woman saw that the tree was good for food, and that it was a delight to the eyes, and that the tree was desirable to make one wise, she took from its fruit and ate; and she gave also to her husband with her, and he ate.

7 Then the eyes of both of them were opened, and they knew that they were naked; and they sewed fig leaves together and made themselves loin coverings.

Similarities:

_____

_____

_____

Read 1 John 2:15-17. Mark the words *world*, *lust*, and *love*.

What's Love Got to Do with It?

1 John 2

¹⁵ Do not love the world nor the things in the world. If anyone loves the world, the love of the Father is not in him.
¹⁶ For all that is in the world, the lust of the flesh and the lust of the eyes and the boastful pride of life, is not from the Father, but is from the world.
¹⁷ The world is passing away, and also its lusts; but the one who does the will of God lives forever.

How does this passage describe what happened to David and Eve? Did they have a choice? What does love have to do with this?

_____

_____

_____

David's actions went from bad to worse. Bathsheba informed David that she was pregnant, and the games began. David sent for Uriah, encouraging him to spend time with his wife so it would appear that the unborn child was actually Uriah's. That plan did not work; Uriah was loyal to his fellow warriors and would not go to his wife while the army lay in temporary shelters, camping out in open fields.

David tried to manipulate Uriah by getting him drunk so he would spend time with his wife. That did

Looking for Love in the Wrong Place

not work either. I find it interesting that Uriah, a Hittite in Israel's army, had one wife, and his loyalty to Israel caused him to control himself and not have sex with her, whereas David, a man of the tribe of Judah, had a palace full of wives yet he did not control himself but instead took another man's wife.

No amount of persuasion could get Uriah to spend the night at home with his wife. So King David sent Uriah back to the battle with a note that would jeopardize Israel's military forces and put an end to his own life. Joab, the commander of Israel's army, was ordered to put Uriah in the front line of the battle, then pull the rest of the warriors back so that Uriah would be killed. That should solve David's problem, right?

Joab did as he was ordered. So Uriah, one of David's "mighty men," died in battle at David's command because David refused to die to his flesh. Not much love in that action.

David married Bathsheba, and about nine months after the hot-bath experience, a baby boy was born. Can you imagine the talk around the palace? Uriah killed in battle, his wife married to the king, and a few months later, a new baby is born. But eventually everything settled into place. People went on with their lives and soon forgot all the drama.

Life goes on, but God does not forget. He sent Nathan the prophet to confront the king about his sin.

What's Love Got to Do with It?

Nathan told a story that was analogous to David's situation. It was about a man with many sheep who stole the one beloved sheep of another man. It did not take the king long to come up with the required restitution for someone who would do such a shameful thing.

Read the following verses and underline what God did for David, and from verse 9 record the sin.

2 Samuel 12

7 Nathan then said to David, "You are the man! Thus says the LORD of Israel, 'It is I who anointed you king over Israel and it is I who delivered you from the hand of Saul.

8 'I also gave you your master's house and your master's wives into your care, and I gave you the house of Israel and Judah; and if that had been too little, I would have added to you many more things like these!

9 'Why have you despised the word of the LORD by doing evil in His sight? You have struck down Uriah the Hittite with the sword, have taken his wife to be your wife, and have killed him with the sword of the sons of Ammon.'"

David's sin:

_____

_____

_____

Looking for Love in the Wrong Place

Read the following verses and underline the consequences of David's sin.

2 Samuel 12

¹⁰ Now therefore, the sword shall never depart from your house, because you have despised Me and have taken the wife of Uriah the Hittite to be your wife.
¹¹ "Thus says the LORD, 'Behold, I will raise up evil against you from your own household; I will even take your wives before your eyes and give them to your companion, and he will lie with your wives in broad daylight.
¹² 'Indeed you did it secretly, but I will do this thing before all Israel, and under the sun.'"

List the consequences:

1.
_____
_____
_____

2.
_____
_____
_____

What's Love Got to Do with It?

3.
_____

_____

_____

Go back and read verses 9-10 and record below what David despised.

_____

_____

_____

Word Study

The Hebrew word for *despised* is *bazah* (baw-zaw'). It means "a primitive root; to disesteem:– despise, disdain, contemptible, think to scorn, a vile person."

David despised God's word and he despised God when he chose to do what he wanted to do instead of what he knew to be right. This is the same word used when Michal "despised" David as he danced before the Lord and when Esau "despised" his birthright. Unlike Michal and Esau, who did not repent, David did.

Underline David's response to Nathan and the occasion that was opened to the enemies of the Lord. There is also one more consequence; record it below.

Looking for Love in the Wrong Place

¹³ Then David said to Nathan, "I have sinned against the LORD." And Nathan said to David, "The LORD also has taken away your sin; you shall not die.

¹⁴ "However, because by this deed you have given occasion to the enemies of the LORD to blaspheme, the child also that is born to you shall surely die."

¹⁵ So Nathan went to his house. Then the LORD struck the child that Uriah's widow bore to David, so that he was very sick.

_____

_____

_____

Consequence #4:

Just as Nathan said, the child died and the last consequence was the first to occur. However, God is gracious. Read 2 Samuel 12:24-15. Mark *David, Bathsheba,* and *Lord.*

2 Samuel 12

²⁴ Then David comforted his wife Bathsheba, and went in to her and lay with her; and she gave birth to a son, and he named him Solomon. Now the LORD loved him

²⁵ and sent word through Nathan the prophet, and he named him Jedidiah for the LORD'S sake.

Describe the relationships between:

What's Love Got to Do with It?

David and Bathsheba

_____

_____

_____

The Lord and Solomon

_____

_____

_____

What was the name given by Nathan and what did it mean?

The man who had caused all her misery brought comfort to Bathsheba and was welcomed into her bed. Perhaps her heartbeat was with David's in asking God's forgiveness for her role in all this. Certainly God's forgiveness is clearly seen in giving them another son, Jedidiah, meaning "for the Lord's sake" or "beloved of God." The son, Solomon, became the next king of Israel and the wisest man on earth.

Read David's request for forgiveness in Psalm 51:1-4, underlining *sin* and its pronouns.

Psalms 51

[1] <<For the choir director. A Psalm of David, when Nathan the prophet came to him, after he had gone in to Bathsheba.>> Be gracious to me, O God, according to Your lovingkindness; According to the

Looking for Love in the Wrong Place

greatness of Your compassion blot out my transgressions.

² Wash me thoroughly from my iniquity and cleanse me from my sin.

³ For I know my transgressions, and my sin is ever before me.

⁴ Against You, You only, I have sinned and done what is evil in Your sight, so that You are justified when You speak and blameless when You judge.

David uses three Hebrew words to describe his sin:

(a) *pesha*: to transgress, to rebel or defy authority
(b) *chattaah:* to sin, miss the mark or miss the way
(c) *avon:* iniquity, guilt, perverse

David acknowledged all areas of his sin. He wanted total and complete forgiveness. He had defied the authority of God, his actions were perverse or twisted, and he had missed the mark of God's divine standard.

David knew enough about himself to admit, confess, and repent of his sin. He knew enough about God to ask for forgiveness on the basis of God's lovingkindness (His favor, kindness, and unfailing love) as well as God's compassion (mercy and tender love). Throwing himself on the mercy of God, David sought God's tender and unfailing love in the midst of his sin situation. Can you see why he is called a man after God's own heart? Can you see what love has to do with this?

What's Love Got to Do with It?

Over the years, as Solomon grew up in the palace, the consequences of David's sin with Bathsheba hit the king from within his own household. One son, Amnon, raped his sister Tamar. Absolom killed Amnon for what he had done to his sister.

Absolom also sought to usurp David's authority and set himself up as the king of Israel. He stole the hearts of the people and gathered some of David's key people to himself (e.g., Ahithophel, David's counselor and Bathsheba's grandfather). Some were invited, but the conspiracy was so strong that many others followed the self-appointed king.

When David heard the news, he quickly left the palace to escape from his son. Absolom, under counsel from Ahithophel, lay with his father's concubines in broad daylight. Absolom committed murder and adultery in his father's house, and all of Israel knew. In those days, the advice of Ahithophel was as if one inquired of the word of God. So when Absolom rejected his advice on how to pursue and kill David, and took the advice of another, Ahithophel committed suicide.

When Absolom was killed in battle, David returned to his house to rule the nation Israel. Bathsheba bore him three more sons in addition to Solomon and seemed to become a devoted mother, a trusted companion, and a highly respected woman.

When David became old and another of his sons sought to appoint himself as king, Bathsheba interceded

Looking for Love in the Wrong Place

for their son, Solomon. Read the following verses, marking *David*, *Bathsheba*, and *Solomon*.

1 Kings 1

17 She [Bathsheba] said to him, "My lord, you swore to your maidservant by the LORD your God, saying, 'Surely your son Solomon shall be king after me and he shall sit on my throne.'

18 "Now, behold, Adonijah is king; and now, my lord the king, you do not know it.

19 "He has sacrificed oxen and fatlings and sheep in abundance, and has invited all the sons of the king and Abiathar the priest and Joab the commander of the army, but he has not invited Solomon your servant.

20 "As for you now, my lord the king, the eyes of all Israel are on you, to tell them who shall sit on the throne of my lord the king after him.

21 "Otherwise it will come about, as soon as my lord the king sleeps with his fathers, that I and my son Solomon will be considered offenders."

What is Bathsheba's request? Why does she ask for this?

_____

_____

_____

Read the following verses, underlining *Nathan*.

What's Love Got to Do with It?

1 Kings 1

²² Behold, while she was still speaking with the king, Nathan the prophet came in.

²³ They told the king, saying, "Here is Nathan the prophet." And when he came in before the king, he prostrated himself before the king with his face to the ground.

²⁴ Then Nathan said, "My lord the king, have you said, 'Adonijah shall be king after me, and he shall sit on my throne'?

²⁵ "For he has gone down today and has sacrificed oxen and fatlings and sheep in abundance, and has invited all the king's sons and the commanders of the army and Abiathar the priest, and behold, they are eating and drinking before him; and they say, 'Long live King Adonijah!'

²⁶ "But me, even me your servant, and Zadok the priest and Benaiah the son of Jehoiada and your servant Solomon, he has not invited.

²⁷ "Has this thing been done by my lord the king, and you have not shown to your servants who should sit on the throne of my lord the king after him?"

What is Nathan's request?

_____

_____

_____

Looking for Love in the Wrong Place

It is interesting to note that Nathan the prophet, the one who confronted David about the sin involving Uriah and Bathsheba, is in agreement with her about who should sit on the throne. It certainly appears she has won his respect.

David once again listens to a wise woman. Mark *David, Bathsheba,* and *Solomon.* Underline what God had redeemed David from.

> **1 Kings 1**
>
> ²⁸ Then King David said, "Call Bathsheba to me." And she came into the king's presence and stood before the king.
> ²⁹ The king vowed and said, "As the LORD lives, who has redeemed my life from all distress,
> ³⁰ "surely as I vowed to you by the LORD the God of Israel, saying, 'Your son Solomon shall be king after me, and he shall sit on my throne in my place'; I will indeed do so this day."
> ³¹ Then Bathsheba bowed with her face to the ground, and prostrated herself before the king and said, "May my lord King David live forever."

As David promised and as God had purposed, Solomon became the king of Israel. That marked the beginning of the fulfillment of God's promise to David that someone from his line would always sit on the throne and that his house would endure forever. This promise, this covenant, was made by God to David before the

What's Love Got to Do with It?

Bathsheba/Uriah affair. God kept his covenant promise even though David sinned. Not one of the promises that the Lord made to David failed. Not one!

Wife of King David and the mother of King Solomon, Bathsheba has a special place in the genealogy of Jesus Christ, Son of David, Seed of Abraham, of the tribe of Judah, Savior of the world, forever on the throne.

Now we know that love had everything to do with it. Mark the words *love* and *believe* in the following verses.

> "For God so loved the world, that He gave His only begotten Son, that whoever believes in Him shall not perish, but have eternal life.
> —John 3:16

> We have come to know and have believed the love which God has for us. God is love, and the one who abides in love abides in God, and God abides in him.
> —1 John 4:16

Do you believe it?

_____

_____

_____

Looking for Love in the Wrong Place

Selah…Think about it.

1. List the sins that you see in the account of David and Bathsheba.

   _____

   _____

   _____

2. Should David have known better? (Deut. 17:14-20; Ex. 20:14)

   _____

   _____

   _____

3. What did you learn about God in this lesson?

   _____

   _____

   _____

4. Read Psalm 32, which was written by David, and notice his use of the different Hebrew words for sin. What would you say that he knew about God, about sin, and about forgiveness?

   _____

   _____

   _____

Chapter 4

LOVE ABUSED
AMNON AND TAMAR

What is it that makes a person lose control of his or her senses in the name of love? Some people in love cannot seem to think clearly and make intelligent decisions. Some do irrational things they would not do under ordinary circumstances. Many do not consider the consequences of their behavior. Sometimes you have to wonder if love has anything to do with it.

Amnon, born in Hebron, was the first son of David, the king of Israel. Amnon was a strong young man but easily influenced by his friends. Controlled by his flesh, yet frustrated, because some things were out of his control.

Tamar was the beautiful virgin sister of Absalom, the third son of David. Amnon and Tamar were brother and sister. They had the same father, different mothers, but

Looking for Love in the Wrong Place

all in the family. Read the following verses and underline the problem and the proposed solution.

2 Samuel 13

¹ Now it was after this that Absalom the son of David had a beautiful sister whose name was Tamar, and Amnon the son of David loved her.

² Amnon was so frustrated because of his sister Tamar that he made himself ill, for she was a virgin, and it seemed hard to Amnon to do anything to her.

³ But Amnon had a friend whose name was Jonadab, the son of Shimeah, David's brother; and Jonadab was a very shrewd man.

⁴ He said to him, "O son of the king, why are you so depressed morning after morning? Will you not tell me?" Then Amnon said to him, "I am in love with Tamar, the sister of my brother Absalom."

Virgins were usually protected and diligently watched. Amnon seemed more concerned about being able to get to her than the fact that she was a virgin and his sister. Cousin Jonadab, shrewd and ready to offer the son of the king a workable solution, moved without hesitation.

Word Study

The Hebrew word for *love* is *ahab*. It means "to have affection for (sexually or otherwise):–love, like, friend."

Love Abused

Mark the suggested solution and Amnon's response.

2 Samuel 13

5 Jonadab then said to him, "Lie down on your bed and pretend to be ill; when your father comes to see you, say to him, 'Please let my sister Tamar come and give me some food to eat, and let her prepare the food in my sight, that I may see it and eat from her hand.'"

6 So Amnon lay down and pretended to be ill; when the king came to see him, Amnon said to the king, "Please let my sister Tamar come and make me a couple of cakes in my sight, that I may eat from her hand."

7 Then David sent to the house for Tamar, saying, "Go now to your brother Amnon's house, and prepare food for him."

Amnon, controlled by his emotions, did not count the cost of this manipulative counsel. Amnon did not hesitate to put the plan into action.

Obviously not a man of integrity, Amnon begins to live the lie and is on a downward spiral to destruction. The plot thickens. Read on!

Underline Amnon's action and double underline Tamar's actions.

Looking for Love in the Wrong Place

2 Samuel 13

⁸ So Tamar went to her brother Amnon's house, and he was lying down. And she took dough, kneaded it, made cakes in his sight, and baked the cakes.

⁹ She took the pan and dished them out before him, but he refused to eat. And Amnon said, "Have everyone go out from me." So everyone went out from him.

¹⁰ Then Amnon said to Tamar, "Bring the food into the bedroom, that I may eat from your hand." So Tamar took the cakes which she had made and brought them into the bedroom to her brother Amnon.

¹¹ When she brought them to him to eat, he took hold of her and said to her, "Come, lie with me, my sister."

Tamar obediently prepared the food. This action quickly accelerated with no one in the house except the two of them in the bedroom. His real reason for calling her came out into the open. Tamar understood the consequences, tried hard to dissuade her brother, and offered an interesting solution.

But he did not listen. With raging passion, totally out of control, he missed the opportunity to repent and turn from evil. He did not even tell her he loved her.

Read the following passage. Underline the consequences and the solution Tamar offered and list them below.

Love Abused

2 Samuel 13

¹² But she answered him, "No, my brother, do not violate me, for such a thing is not done in Israel; do not do this disgraceful thing!
¹³ "As for me, where could I get rid of my reproach? And as for you, you will be like one of the fools in Israel. Now therefore, please speak to the king, for he will not withhold me from you."

Tamar's response is no! List her rationale and her solution:

_____

_____

_____

Do you see any of Tamar's rationale in the following passages? Should Amnon have known these passages? Underline the consequences of Amnon's action in the following verses.

Leviticus 20

¹⁷ If there is a man who takes his sister, his father's daughter or his mother's daughter, so that he sees her nakedness and she sees his nakedness, it is a disgrace; and they shall be cut off in the sight of the sons of their people. He has uncovered his sister's nakedness; he bears his guilt.

Looking for Love in the Wrong Place

Deuteronomy 22

²⁵ But if in the field the man finds the girl who is engaged, and the man forces her and lies with her, then only the man who lies with her shall die.

Deuteronomy 27

²² "Cursed is he who lies with his sister, the daughter of his father or of his mother." And all the people shall say, "Amen."

Tamar knew the consequences. She understood clearly, and Amnon should have as well. But Amnon lost his reasoning. The lust of the flesh was ruling, and he was totally out of control. Tamar pleaded with him for her sake and for his sake, but he would not listen. He overpowered her and forced her. He raped her!

Hundreds of women could echo the pleas and pain of Tamar. Women unwillingly forced into the sexual act against their will. What does love have to do with this?

A dream come true for Amnon. He's now a happy man, right? Not! Underline Amnon's actions and double underline Tamar's response.

2 Samuel 13

¹⁴ However, he would not listen to her; since he was stronger than she, he violated her and lay with her.

Love Abused

¹⁵ Then Amnon hated her with a very great hatred; for the hatred with which he hated her was greater than the love with which he had loved her. And Amnon said to her, "Get up, go away!"
¹⁶ But she said to him, "No, because this wrong in sending me away is greater than the other that you have done to me!" Yet he would not listen to her.
¹⁷ Then he called his young man who attended him and said, "Now throw this woman out of my presence, and lock the door behind her."
¹⁸ Now she had on a long-sleeved garment; for in this manner the virgin daughters of the king dressed themselves in robes. Then his attendant took her out and locked the door behind her.
¹⁹ Tamar put ashes on her head and tore her long-sleeved garment which was on her; and she put her hand on her head and went away, crying aloud as she went.

He hated her more than he had loved her. He raped her, and he's the one who's angry. What is that all about? The same woman, who ruled his emotions leading to such outrageous passion, somehow became the enemy. She was now totally and completely odious to him.

Look at the definition of the word *hate* below. According to the law in Leviticus and Deuteronomy that we looked at earlier, he is cursed and has a death sentence on his head.

Looking for Love in the Wrong Place

Word Study

The Hebrew word for *hate* is *sane* (saw-nay'), meaning "to hate (personally):–enemy, foe, (be) hate (-ful, -r), odious, utterly."

Although Amnon initiated all the action, can you see why he would see her as an enemy? Has his reasoning returned? Does he finally realize he was wrong and the deep consequences for his sin?

Amnon had become captive to his own trap of deception. Read the following passage, underlining all you see about lust and where it leads.

James 1

^{14} But each one is tempted when he is carried away and enticed by his own lust.

^{15} Then when lust has conceived, it gives birth to sin; and when sin is accomplished, it brings forth death.

^{16} Do not be deceived, my beloved brethren.

Read and underline what the Lord says about Israel's refusal to listen and their lack of obedience. God wanted to fill them, satisfy them, and protect them. Circle what God wanted them to do and what they actually did. Mark what God did because of their heart condition.

Love Abused

Psalms 81

¹⁰ I, the LORD, am your God, Who brought you up from the land of Egypt; Open your mouth wide and I will fill it.

¹¹ But My people did not listen to My voice, And Israel did not obey Me.

¹² So I gave them over to the stubbornness of their heart, To walk in their own devices.

¹³ Oh that My people would listen to Me, That Israel would walk in My ways!

¹⁴ I would quickly subdue their enemies And turn My hand against their adversaries.

¹⁵ Those who hate the LORD would pretend obedience to Him, And their time of punishment would be forever.

¹⁶ But I would feed you with the finest of the wheat, And with honey from the rock I would satisfy you.

Read and underline the instruction. Do you see why fleshly lusts are a problem?

_____

_____

_____

1 Peter 2

¹¹ Beloved, I urge you as aliens and strangers to abstain from fleshly lusts which wage war against the soul.

Looking for Love in the Wrong Place

Amnon told Tamar to get up and get out. But she was persistent and would not leave without telling Amnon once again how wrong all of his actions were and that he was further compounding the problem. But once again he would not listen.

Passion out of control, he threw her out. Surely he would not get away with this. He had raped her; she lost her virginity; she was shamed; her life would be changed forever and *he had her thrown out!*

Those who look for love in the wrong place find themselves in places they wish they had not gone, doing what they should not have done. They invariably subject themselves and others to deep and sometimes irreversible hurt. Amnon is in that place, and unless he repents, judgment is on the way. Read on!

Mark every reference to *Amnon, Tamar,* and *Absalom.* Look for a time period in the passage and underline how Absalom feels about Amnon.

2 Samuel 13

[20] Then Absalom her brother said to her, "Has Amnon your brother been with you? But now keep silent, my sister, he is your brother; do not take this matter to heart." So Tamar remained and was desolate in her brother Absalom's house.

[21] Now when King David heard of all these matters, he was very angry.

[22] But Absalom did not speak to Amnon either good or bad; for Absalom hated Amnon because he had violated his sister Tamar.

Love Abused

²³ Now it came about after two full years that Absalom had sheepshearers in Baal-hazor, which is near Ephraim, and Absalom invited all the king's sons.
²⁴ Absalom came to the king and said, "Behold now, your servant has sheepshearers; please let the king and his servants go with your servant."
²⁵ But the king said to Absalom, "No, my son, we should not all go, for we will be burdensome to you." Although he urged him, he would not go, but blessed him.
²⁶ Then Absalom said, "If not, please let my brother Amnon go with us." And the king said to him, "Why should he go with you?"
²⁷ But when Absalom urged him, he let Amnon and all the king's sons go with him.

What was Absalom's cue that Amnon may have been the cause of Tamar's grief? Record David's response to this terrible situation. Describe Tamar's reaction to the situation. Describe Absalom's plan.

David's response:

_____

_____

_____

Tamar's reaction:

_____

Looking for Love in the Wrong Place

_____

_____

Absalom's plan:

_____

_____

_____

Read and mark every reference to *Absalom, Amnon,* and *Jonadab*.

2 Samuel 13

²⁸ Absalom commanded his servants, saying, "See now, when Amnon's heart is merry with wine, and when I say to you, 'Strike Amnon,' then put him to death. Do not fear; have not I myself commanded you? Be courageous and be valiant."

²⁹ The servants of Absalom did to Amnon just as Absalom had commanded. Then all the king's sons arose and each mounted his mule and fled.

³⁰ Now it was while they were on the way that the report came to David, saying, "Absalom has struck down all the king's sons, and not one of them is left."

³¹ Then the king arose, tore his clothes and lay on the ground; and all his servants were standing by with clothes torn.

³² Jonadab, the son of Shimeah, David's brother, responded, "Do not let my lord suppose they have put to death all the young men, the king's sons,

Love Abused

for Amnon alone is dead; because by the intent of Absalom this has been determined since the day that he violated his sister Tamar.
33 "Now therefore, do not let my lord the king take the report to heart, namely, 'all the king's sons are dead,' for only Amnon is dead."

Love, hate, deception, rape, abuse, bitterness, anger, revenge, and murder, all in the royal family! How long had Absalom been holding a grudge and planning the death of his brother?

Look who reappeared and brought King David the news of the death of his son Amnon. It was Jonadab, Amnon's friend, who counseled him about Tamar.

David did not punish Amnon, but Absalom took his revenge, digging a hole for himself. Absalom was running the show. He finally had things in control—or so he thought. In reality, he was out of control. Tamar, the beautiful princess, went to live with her brother Absalom, ashamed and desolate. How many wrongs make a right?

God offers help to both victims and criminals. Whether you believe it or not, you are beloved of God. He desires complete healing and wholeness for you. Your sorrow is not beyond healing; there is a balm in Gilead. God has a miraculous system of deliverance that is activated when you trust Him. If you have been trying to solve your own problem, forget it. The Word says (2

Looking for Love in the Wrong Place

Chron. 20:6) that power and might are in God's hand and no one can stand against Him.

In 2 Corinthians 12 God makes a promise: "My grace is sufficient for you, for power is perfected in weakness." So you can rest in the sovereignty of God. He is in control and His solution is best. When you trust Him, you can have the assurance that God will fulfill His purpose for you and will perfect whatever concerns you.

Everyone is influenced by past and present circumstances, but none who trust God have to be controlled by them. The bondage-breaking process happens when you trust God and become conformed by the renewing of your mind. When the new comes in, the old is tossed out. Whatever situation you are in or whatever has happened to you in the past, Jesus wants to set you free to live in His ways and He will never break His lovingkindness for you. Get to know the truth of God, really know it, for it will make you free!

Psalm 89

[33] But I will not break off My lovingkindness from him, Nor deal falsely in My faithfulness.
[34] My covenant I will not violate, Nor will I alter the utterance of My lips.

Love Abused

Selah…Think about it.

1. What can you do with passion that is totally out of control? Is there ever a time when "I just couldn't help it" would be an appropriate response? Based on what you have learned from this lesson, make a list of actions to take to control your passions.

   _____

   _____

   _____

2. If the love of God had been in Amnon's life, what changes would you expect? What changes would there be in Absalom's life?

   _____

   _____

   _____

3. What is the one major thing you can do to be free of past pain and trouble that has had long-term, negative influences in your life?

   _____

   _____

   _____

Looking for Love in the Wrong Place

4. How would you explain to someone how to look for love that will last and the impact that love can have on that person's life and the lives of others?

　　_____

　　_____

　　_____

Chapter 5

BLINDED BY LOVE
SAMSON'S LIFE OF LUST AND LOVE

It was the time of the judges, a very dark period in the history of Israel, a time when there was no king in Israel and everyone was doing what was right in his or her own eyes, a time when the people did not know God or the work He had done for His children.

During this almost four-hundred-year period, judges ruled Israel. Israel forsook God, played the harlot after other gods, and refused to listen to their judges. The people found themselves in a nonstop cycle of sin. The sons of Israel would sin and God would send in an oppressor, usually a nearby country. After a time when it seemed they could take it no longer, Israel would repent and cry unto the Lord and He would send a judge to deliver them. God would free them from oppression for the remainder of the judge's life. When that judge

Looking for Love in the Wrong Place

died, the people would sin again and the cycle would start all over.

Israel had the wealth of the promises of God and yet they were morally degraded and spiritually bankrupt; they lived in spiritual poverty. Israel was a corrupt and oppressed nation in a downward spiral of sin.

During these days God raised up Samson as a judge and deliverer. Samson was a very famous judge, well known for his strength but also well known for his weakness for women.

The announcement of Samson's birth by an angel was a wonderful surprise to his parents, who had no other children. They were of the tribe of Dan and lived adjacent to the Philistines. Samson was to be a Nazirite from the womb until the day of his death, and he was never to cut his hair. (The vow of a Nazirite was to drink no strong drink, wine or grape juice; to eat no fresh or dried grapes; nor go near a dead person). Samson's separation was for a lifetime; he was to be set apart as holy for God all the days of his life.

Read the following verse, underlining Samson's purpose.

Judges 13

[5] For behold, you shall conceive and give birth to a son, and no razor shall come upon his head, for the boy shall be a Nazirite to God from the womb;

Blinded by Love

and he shall begin to deliver Israel from the hands of the Philistines.

At this point in the life of the nation, Israel had once again done evil in the sight of the Lord, so God gave them over to the hands of the Philistines. For the past forty years the Philistines had ruled over Israel and been their oppressors. Samson's purpose was to begin to deliver Israel from the Philistines.

LOVE LOST

Samson grew up and was blessed by God. As time went on, he began to make some bad choices, and God allowed it. One day he saw a woman of the Philistines and decided to take her as his wife for no apparent reason other than she looked good. God's command not to marry outside the Jewish nation (Deut. 7:3) was not enough to persuade Samson to change his mind. His father talked to him, trying to encourage him to take a wife from among the Israelites, but to no avail.

Samson, one of the strongest men in the Bible, had an area of weakness that God used over and over again to accomplish His purpose. Handsome, determined, and very strong willed, Samson would not yield to his father's counsel or to God's command. Although chosen and set apart for God, obviously reared under the influence of godly parents, Samson refused to acknowledge God or listen to his parents and married her anyway. Samson,

Looking for Love in the Wrong Place

although set apart for God, did not consult with God, nor did he seem to desire to please Him. He sought only to please his own flesh. He wanted her and married her because she looked good.

Yielding to the flesh marks the beginning of working against the will of God. A major component of "looking for love in the wrong place" is yielding to the flesh against the will of God.

What happens if you marry the wrong person, going against the commands of God? What, if any, warning does God give for us today? Read the following verses, underlining what God says about relationships.

2 Corinthians 6

¹⁴ Do not be bound together with unbelievers; for what partnership have righteousness and lawlessness, or what fellowship has light with darkness?
¹⁵ Or what harmony has Christ with Belial, or what has a believer in common with an unbeliever?
¹⁶ Or what agreement has the temple of God with idols? For we are the temple of the living God; just as God said, "I will dwell in them and walk among them; and I will be their god, and they shall be my people.
¹⁷ "Therefore, come out from their midst and be separate," says the Lord. "And do not touch what is unclean; and I will welcome you.

Light has nothing in common with darkness. They cannot coexist in the same place. When animals of two

Blinded by Love

different sizes are yoked together, the yoke chafes both animals and makes their labor ineffective. An ox and a donkey, for example, are not only different sizes, they have different bone structures. A yoke suited for one will rub and eventually wound the other.

We have nothing in common with those who do not believe in or live according to God's commands. If God has changed your heart and has given you His Holy Spirit, who causes you to walk in His commands, there will always be conflict with those who do not know God. You can never have a total commitment to such a person. When the love of Christ is in you, your inherent and internal loyalty to God will always rise to the top.

Samson, on his way to talk to the girl, saw a lion and killed it under the power of the Spirit, without a weapon in his hands. He did not seem to know what kind of power he had or that the Spirit of God was working in him. Like David, he learned to fight beasts before he fought the Philistines.

When Samson returned to the same location some time later, a swarm of bees had taken up residence in the carcass. As he passed by, he looked, perhaps remembering the magnificent feat God had performed through him in that spot. He took a handful of honey and ate it as he traveled. He took some of the honey to his parents, though he did not tell them where it came from.

Samson seems to have forgotten the law (Lev. 11:27) that if someone touches something unclean, that person

Looking for Love in the Wrong Place

becomes unclean. Nor does he seem to remember that because he was a Nazirite, he was not to touch anything dead. Or did he really forget? After all, he was living in the time of the judges, when everyone was doing what was right in his or her own eyes.

As was the custom, when the marriage festivities began Samson proposed a riddle to his thirty Philistine companions:

> "Out of the eater came something to eat, And out of the strong came something sweet."
> —Judg.14:14

None of his friends could come close to solving the riddle. His new wife, under threat of her life and that of her family, pressed Samson with tears and "If you love me…" He finally gave her the solution to the riddle, and she revealed the secret to the men of her family. Though Samson didn't know it at the time, all this led directly to God's purpose for Samson, which was to begin to deliver the children of Israel from the hands of the Philistines.

Losing the challenge required Samson to provide thirty changes of clothes to the winners of his riddle. He went to another city, where the Spirit of the Lord came upon him, and he killed thirty men, took the spoil, and paid his debt. Samson responded out of the flesh and out of his anger. However, God used him as His

Blinded by Love

executioner and the occasion was used to accomplish His purpose.

Samson was so angry, he left his wife and returned to his father's house. She was then given as a wife to a companion who had once been his friend. One wrong choice leads to another and another and another. Samson had allowed "love" to so blind him that he made foolish choices, defiantly breaking God's commands, including God's selected Nazirite separation for his life. The result to Samson was betrayal, pain, hurt, friends who deceived him, and a wife who deserted him. When your weakness becomes your guide, pain becomes your companion.

After a while, Samson decided to return to his wife. It was during wheat harvest, April or May, a very dry time of the year. It did not take him long to learn that his wife had been given to his companion. The girl's father tried to offer a younger sister to Samson, which would have caused him to break another of God's laws (Lev. 18:18). He did not fall for it; however, anger and the desire for vengeance drove him in another wrong direction. He went to war.

Samson came up with his own unique battle plan. He gathered three hundred foxes, tied their tails together, and put torches in the middle of their tails. When he had set fire to the torches, he turned the foxes loose in the Philistines' standing grain fields (fields that had been reaped and gathered). Their fields burned and the Philistines were outraged. Discovering Samson as the

Looking for Love in the Wrong Place

offender, they burned the woman and her father. The very thing that she had feared (Judg. 14:15) came upon her and her father.

Samson, still looking for satisfaction, sought revenge, and God again worked to accomplish His purpose. Samson struck them with a great and merciless slaughter. Then he went down and lived in the top of the rock in Etam, not far from home. The Philistines camped out in Judah, looking for Samson.

A three-thousand-man delegation went to see Samson. The men of Judah, not willing to risk their lives for Samson, decided to turn him over to the Philistines. They reminded him that they were under the rule of the Philistines and asked if they could bind him and turn him in. It is interesting that they would rather turn Samson over to the enemies than fight along with him to get the nation out of an oppressed situation.

Samson expressed no remorse, saying, "As they did to me, so I have done to them." The men of Judah agreed not to kill him but to bind him and turn him over to the Philistines. But God intervened, for the Spirit of the Lord came upon him and the ropes practically melted from his wrists. He found a fresh jawbone of a donkey and killed one thousand Philistines.

What a war! Some here and some there, they fell on every side. Even in Samson's rebellion, God fought for the Israelites, using an appointed vessel to accomplish His purpose. "One man of you shall chase a thousand…" (Jos.23:10).

Blinded by Love

How did Samson get from wanting a girl in Timnah to running for his life, chased by his enemies, rejected and unappreciated by his people, living on top of a rock, consumed and eaten up by vengeance? It started with a woman, with love, with a look, a look in the wrong place.

LOVE OR LUST?

Samson judged Israel for twenty years. During those years, making provision for the flesh was a common thing for him. Whenever he wanted a woman he went after her. One day, in an area near the Mediterranean Sea, he went to Gaza, capital of the largest of the Philistine cities. Pride of life was not his weakness, but lust of the eyes was his frequent partner. In the city of Gaza, Samson saw a harlot and went in to her. Once again a look, then lust ensnared Samson, and now he is headed for trouble.

Read the following verses.

James 1

¹⁴ But each one is tempted when he is carried away and enticed by his own lust.
¹⁵ Then when lust has conceived, it gives birth to sin; and when sin is accomplished, it brings forth death.

Samson was so enticed and carried away by lust that he endangered his own life and essentially wrote

Looking for Love in the Wrong Place

his own death warrant. Looking for love in the wrong place, he was discovered by the Gazites, who made plans to capture him.

For some reason, they decided to wait at the city gate until the morning light and kill him then. The gates of the city were shut; the guards were set, everything and everyone was quiet. They thought they had him in a trap, imprisoned in the city. About midnight, Samson arose and made his way toward the gate of the city, probably finding the guards asleep. He did not break open the gates, but plucked up the posts, gates, bars, and all. Large, strong, and heavy, yet he carried them on his shoulders several miles, up to the top of a hill, to a mountain opposite Hebron, giving proof of the great strength God had given him.

The instructions of God are clear, His promises are available, and freedom is well within reach. Yet many today, young and old alike, are living like Samson. Simply knowing the Word is not good enough; it must be lived out. Broken people trying to fill broken cisterns that do not hold water, these are people who attend church but do not really know why Christ came. These people read and study His Word, but do not walk in the freedom it provides, having a form of godliness but denying its power (2 Tim. 3:5). You cannot yield to sin without exposing yourself to danger and destruction.

Blinded by Love

John 8

³⁴ Jesus answered them, "Truly, truly, I say to you, everyone who commits sin is the slave of sin.

Samson was a slave to his sin, yet God continued to use him to accomplish his purpose, but not for always.

LOVE LOCKS

Then comes another city, Sorek, and another woman, Delilah. Samson's strength was well known throughout the land. He knew it and the people knew it. Also well known was his love for women. Seeking to conquer the unconquerable Samson, the Philistines of this city used his weakness (his love for women) to determine where his strength was found.

Read the following passage, looking for Delilah's request and Samson's response. Also underline the words *strength* and *bound*.

Judges 16

⁴ After this it came about that he loved a woman in the valley of Sorek, whose name was Delilah.
⁵ The lords of the Philistines came up to her and said to her, "Entice him, and see where his great strength lies and how we may overpower him that we may bind him to afflict him. Then we will each give you eleven hundred pieces of silver."

Looking for Love in the Wrong Place

⁶ So Delilah said to Samson, "Please tell me where your great strength is and how you may be bound to afflict you."

⁷ Samson said to her, "If they bind me with seven fresh cords that have not been dried, then I will become weak and be like any other man."

⁸ Then the lords of the Philistines brought up to her seven fresh cords that had not been dried, and she bound him with them.

⁹ Now she had men lying in wait in an inner room. And she said to him, "The Philistines are upon you, Samson!" But he snapped the cords as a string of tow snaps when it touches fire. So his strength was not discovered.

Samson, a slave to passion, loved Delilah, but she was willing to sell him out to the highest bidder (1,100 pieces of silver). In verse 7, he seems to realize that "they" (other people) were involved in this scheme. Although bound by cords that could not hold him, Samson was bound in a relationship that held him and led him into a trap that would change his life forever. Blind to it all, he played the deadly game. She manipulated him for money, and when her scheme did not work, she accused him of deception and lying.

Mark the words *deceived, bound,* and *weak.*

Blinded by Love

Judges 16

¹⁰ Then Delilah said to Samson, "Behold, you have deceived me and told me lies; now please tell me how you may be bound."
¹¹ He said to her, "If they bind me tightly with new ropes which have not been used, then I will become weak and be like any other man."
¹² So Delilah took new ropes and bound him with them and said to him, "The Philistines are upon you, Samson!" For the men were lying in wait in the inner room. But he snapped the ropes from his arms like a thread.

I find it almost unbelievable the way he continues to give her information, knowing she is setting him up. Once again he snaps the ropes and breaks free. Delilah, of course, is livid and again calls him a liar. She says she is being deceived and tries again to convince him to tell her the truth. Seductive, manipulative, yet possessing a fascinating quality and an exotic kind of beauty, Delilah persists with her plan of destruction.

Mark the words *strength, bound, deceived, weak,* and *locks.*

Judges 16

¹³ Then Delilah said to Samson, "Up to now you have deceived me and told me lies; tell me how you may be bound." And he said to her, "If you weave

Looking for Love in the Wrong Place

the seven locks of my hair with the web and fasten it with a pin, then I will become weak and be like any other man."

¹⁴ So while he slept, Delilah took the seven locks of his hair and wove them into the web. And she fastened it with the pin and said to him, "The Philistines are upon you, Samson!" But he awoke from his sleep and pulled out the pin of the loom and the web.

The game continues. Samson is free again, but Delilah is persistent. I am not sure why she wanted him to be as weak as any other man, but she keeps asking and he keeps giving her potential solutions. He pretends to reveal the secret of his strength, but each time he tricks her. While he sleeps, she is weaving his locks, trying to unbraid the puzzle.

The third time was the charm. She pulled out the "big guns." What does she say to get him to open his heart to her? Mark the words *love, locks, heart, strength, weak, money,* and *deceived.*

Judges 16

¹⁵ Then she said to him, "How can you say, 'I love you,' when your heart is not with me? You have deceived me these three times and have not told me where your great strength is."

Blinded by Love

¹⁶ It came about when she pressed him daily with her words and urged him, that his soul was annoyed to death.

¹⁷ So he told her all that was in his heart and said to her, "A razor has never come on my head, for I have been a Nazirite to God from my mother's womb. If I am shaved, then my strength will leave me and I will become weak and be like any other man."

¹⁸ When Delilah saw that he had told her all that was in his heart, she sent and called the lords of the Philistines, saying, "Come up once more, for he has told me all that is in his heart." Then the lords of the Philistines came up to her and brought the money in their hands.

¹⁹ She made him sleep on her knees, and called for a man and had him shave off the seven locks of his hair. Then she began to afflict him, and his strength left him.

²⁰ She said, "The Philistines are upon you, Samson!" And he awoke from his sleep and said, "I will go out as at other times and shake myself free." But he did not know that the LORD had departed from him.

Delilah used the love word and pressed him to the mat, annoying his soul. Not knowing what hit him, Samson spilled his guts. He told her of his birth and his consecration to the Lord, of his Nazirite vow; he told her all that was in his heart. She was so sure he had told her the truth this time that the Philistines brought

# Looking for Love in the Wrong Place

the money with them. She was not a tender lover but a cruel enemy!

Locks shaven, she began to afflict him and his strength left him. Samson thought he would get up as he had done before. He did not realize that the Lord had departed and that his strength was gone. The weakness of his heart seemed to surpass the strength of his body. Somehow this love attachment was better to him than the blessings of God in and on his life.

Mark the words *eyes, bound,* and *destroyer.*

Judges 16

21 Then the Philistines seized him and gouged out his eyes; and they brought him down to Gaza and bound him with bronze chains, and he was a grinder in the prison.

22 However, the hair of his head began to grow again after it was shaved off.

23 Now the lords of the Philistines assembled to offer a great sacrifice to Dagon their god, and to rejoice, for they said, "Our god has given Samson our enemy into our hands."

24 When the people saw him, they praised their god, for they said, "Our god has given our enemy into our hands, Even the destroyer of our country, Who has slain many of us."

Not the eyes! To see, to desire, to look, and to lust! The very area of his trouble was gouged out. The strongest man in town was bought and sold for a few

Blinded by Love

pieces of silver because of "eye trouble." From judge and deliverer of a nation to the lowest possible position in the prison of the enemy, all because of a woman and Samson's persistence in looking for love in the wrong place. Delilah is not mentioned again in this passage of Scripture.

The Philistines, celebrating and rejoicing, thought their god had delivered Samson into their hands, but God had a plan. Mark the words *eyes, Lord,* and *God.* Read the definitions given below.

Judges 16

25 It so happened when they were in high spirits, that they said, "Call for Samson, that he may amuse us." So they called for Samson from the prison, and he entertained them. And they made him stand between the pillars.

26 Then Samson said to the boy who was holding his hand, "Let me feel the pillars on which the house rests, that I may lean against them."

27 Now the house was full of men and women, and all the lords of the Philistines were there. And about 3,000 men and women were on the roof looking on while Samson was amusing them.

28 Then Samson called to the LORD and said, "O Lord GOD, please remember me and please strengthen me just this time, O God, that I may at once be avenged of the Philistines for my two eyes."

Looking for Love in the Wrong Place

Word Study

Lord in the Hebrew is *Adonay,* meaning "Lord (proper name of God only)."

GOD in Hebrew is *Yahovih,* "the covenant name for God most prominently known in connection with his relationship with Israel." In verse 28, the name for *GOD*, in all caps is *Yahovih* and has a different meaning when it is translated as *God* (see definition below).

God in Hebrew is *elohiym,* "the supreme God; used to describe God as creator of the heavens and the earth, mighty." Notice that this word for *God* has a different meaning and is not translated with all caps when mentioned the second time in verse 28. Samson is using different names for God as he earnestly prays. Study the definitions to see what difference it makes.

The Philistines, thinking themselves wise, became fools. They called for Samson to entertain them, putting him between the pillars on which the house rested. The house was full of men and women, including many top officials. Additionally, about three thousand were on the roof, watching the entertainment. By this time Samson's hair had grown back and he'd had a lot of time to think. He had talked to God as he had never done before. Samson acknowledged God as creator of all (*elohiym*), used his covenant name (Yahovih), as well as recognizing Him as Lord of all (Adonay). He asked God to remember him and to strengthen him so he could be avenged for his eyes.

Blinded by Love

It is interesting that his strength did not return with the growth of his hair, but with his request to God. What an acknowledgement—that his strength was provided by God to accomplish His will, and was not his own. His request seems at first self-serving except for the "remember me," which drives our thoughts to the thief on the cross.

After recognizing God as the true source of his strength, one more time his strength returned full force and he destroyed the Philistine leaders and many others in the house and on the roof. So much for the entertainment! Mark the words *life* and *death*.

Judges 16
²⁹ Samson grasped the two middle pillars on which the house rested, and braced himself against them, the one with his right hand and the other with his left.
³⁰ And Samson said, "Let me die with the Philistines!" And he bent with all his might so that the house fell on the lords and all the people who were in it. So the dead whom he killed at his death were more than those whom he killed in his life.

Grasping the two pillars, Samson asked to die with the Philistines. This sounds heroic until we remember he got himself in this trouble because of his "eye problems" and his weakness in that area. He did accomplish God's purpose, however, in that during his twenty years

Looking for Love in the Wrong Place

as the ruling judge, he began to deliver Israel from the Philistines.

In this last effort he killed more at his death than he did during his lifetime. Surely there must have been an easier way to carry out God's purpose! Samson did it the hard way, but in the end we see the faith he exercised to conquer kingdoms and that God's strength was perfected in Samson's weakness.

Read the following passage and mark *faith, Samson, weakness,* and *strong.*

Hebrews 11

32 And what more shall I say? For time will fail me if I tell of Gideon, Barak, Samson, Jephthah, of David and Samuel and the prophets,

33 who by faith conquered kingdoms, performed acts of righteousness, obtained promises, shut the mouths of lions,

34 quenched the power of fire, escaped the edge of the sword, from weakness were made strong, became mighty in war, put foreign armies to flight.

Record what you learn about God from Psalm 118:5-9.

Psalm 118

5 From my distress I called upon the LORD; The LORD answered me and set me in a large place.

6 The LORD is for me; I will not fear; What can man do to me?

Blinded by Love

⁷ The LORD is for me among those who help me; Therefore I will look with satisfaction on those who hate me.

⁸ It is better to take refuge in the LORD Than to trust in man.

⁹ It is better to take refuge in the LORD Than to trust in princes.

_____

_____

_____

Looking for Love in the Wrong Place

Selah…Think about it.

1. What common thread do you see in Samson's relationships?

   _____

   _____

   _____

2. What is it about love that blinds or binds a person so much that he or she cannot think clearly? For example, Samson does not seem to be thinking clearly in (1) his response to his wife in Timnah, (2) when he went to Gaza (enemy territory) just for a woman, or (3) when he told Delilah what would make him lose his strength. Is there any hope for a person in this situation? Support your answer with Scriptures.

   _____

   _____

   _____

3. Samson knew he was a Nazirite from his mother's womb, yet he continued to lose focus of his assignment from God. Where is your focus? Look up the following verses and record your findings.

Blinded by Love

a. Proverbs 3:5-6

b. Psalm 32:10

c. Psalm 37:3-8

4. Samson wanted things his own way and seemed to wrestle with his parents, his peers, and his partners. What area in your life do you want to change as a result of studying the life and loves of Samson?

5. Samson was given the ability to perform exploits beyond normal human strength, but he did not always use his abilities wisely. How are you

Looking for Love in the Wrong Place

making wise use of the gifts and talents God has given you?

_____

_____

_____

6. Samson was obviously an angry man. Read the following verses and list the principles for dealing with anger.

James 1:19-20

_____

_____

_____

Ephesians 4:26

_____

_____

_____

Proverbs 10:19

_____

_____

_____

Blinded by Love

7. Underline what you learn about God in Psalm 138:1-8

Psalm 138

¹ I will give You thanks with all my heart; I will sing praises to You before the gods.

² I will bow down toward Your holy temple and give thanks to Your name for Your lovingkindness and Your truth; for You have magnified Your word according to all Your name.

³ On the day I called, You answered me; You made me bold with strength in my soul.

⁴ All the kings of the earth will give thanks to You, O LORD, when they have heard the words of Your mouth.

⁵ And they will sing of the ways of the LORD, for great is the glory of the LORD.

⁶ For though the LORD is exalted, yet He regards the lowly, but the haughty He knows from afar.

⁷ Though I walk in the midst of trouble, You will revive me; You will stretch forth Your hand against the wrath of my enemies, and Your right hand will save me.

⁸ The LORD will accomplish what concerns me; Your lovingkindness, O LORD, is everlasting; do not forsake the works of Your hands.

Chapter 6

LOVE TRANSFORMS
THE WOMAN AT THE WELL

They had been living together for quite some time and it was working out pretty well. Neither one had to totally commit to the other. They thought it better to try out the relationship before getting married. After you've been married five times, doesn't it make sense to try living together before tying the knot, especially with the divorce rate so high? Isn't it better to be sure than to go through those horrible divorce proceedings again? After all, what God joins together no one should put aside, right? Why is it so wrong if it feels so right?

In the city of Sychar (ancient Shechem) of Samaria, there lived a woman. She was well known, but not necessarily well liked. This Samaritan woman was particularly well known by men and had been married at least five times, although she currently had no husband.

Looking for Love in the Wrong Place

Apparently, looking for love had almost become a lifetime adventure for her, without much success.

Typically Jews had no dealings with the Samaritans. During the Assyrian captivity, it is believed that Gentiles (Babylonians, Cuthahians and others) were brought into Samaria and eventually intermarried with the Jews. Their descendants were known as the Samaritans. This racially mixed population had set up on Mount Gerizim a rival temple to the one in Jerusalem, which greatly antagonized the Jews.

Although the Samaritans were idol worshippers, they were eventually taught how to fear the Lord. They feared the Lord, but they also served their own gods. Their pagan practices caused them to be rejected by both Jew and Gentile. Some called them half-breeds. But because Samaria was positioned just north of Judea, between the great sea and Galilee, it fell right along the best route to Jerusalem from Galilee.

Every stop that Jesus made, every road He took, always had a purpose. This stop was no exception. Jesus, becoming weary from His trip from Judea, stopped in Samaria at Jacob's well. It was around noon (Jewish time), and the disciples went off to buy food.

John 4

[7] There came a woman of Samaria to draw water. Jesus said to her, "Give Me a drink."

Love Transforms

⁸ For His disciples had gone away into the city to buy food.
⁹ Therefore the Samaritan woman said to Him, "How is it that You, being a Jew, ask me for a drink since I am a Samaritan woman?" (For Jews have no dealings with Samaritans.)

Jesus clearly got the attention of this woman. She could tell He was a Jew; perhaps there was something about His clothing or His manner of speaking. And yet, he was talking to her, a Samaritan woman. She was surprised that this man, a Jew, would even consider drinking from her water pot.

¹⁰ Jesus answered and said to her, "If you knew the gift of God, and who it is who says to you, 'Give Me a drink,' you would have asked Him, and He would have given you living water."
¹¹ She said to Him, "Sir, You have nothing to draw with and the well is deep; where then do You get that living water?
¹² "You are not greater than our father Jacob, are You, who gave us the well, and drank of it himself and his sons and his cattle?"

Jesus quickly gets to the point of this encounter: living water, the Holy Spirit. As the conversation continues, we can see Jesus is talking about one thing and

Looking for Love in the Wrong Place

she is talking about another. While living water in that day could refer to spring water, the woman is definitely not on the same page. Jesus patiently explains.

John 4

13 Jesus answered and said to her, "Everyone who drinks of this water will thirst again;

14 but whoever drinks of the water that I will give him shall never thirst; but the water that I will give him will become in him a well of water springing up to eternal life."

15 The woman said to Him, "Sir, give me this water, so I will not be thirsty nor come all the way here to draw."

Word Study

The Greek word for *sir* is *kurios* (koo'-ree-os). "From *kuros* (supremacy); supreme in authority, i.e. (as noun) controller; by implication, Master (as a respectful title):– God, Lord, master, Sir."

What a promise! Drink and never thirst again. The transformation begins. She seems to grasp, at least in part, what He is saying. Evidently she traveled a long distance to this well to obtain water. A lifetime supply of living water would cut down her travel time by saving her numerous trips to the well, giving her time to do other things.

Love Transforms

Jesus turned the discussion from living water to eternal life. What hope! She was so excited! He spoke with such confidence she longed to know more. At this point she was ready to take all that He had to offer.

John 4

16 He said to her, "Go, call your husband and come here."

17 The woman answered and said, "I have no husband." Jesus said to her, "You have correctly said, 'I have no husband';

18 for you have had five husbands, and the one whom you now have is not your husband; this you have said truly."

19 The woman said to Him, "Sir, I perceive that You are a prophet.

Suddenly the conversation picked up momentum and Jesus drove her toward the sin issue. He was after more than a drink of water. She gave an answer, but not the complete truth. She was living with a guy, but so what? Most people were doing whatever they wanted to. She had no husband, true, but she had "her man." (The Greek word for "husband" and "man" is the same, and context determines the meaning.)

Jesus tells her about her past husbands and about her current illegal and immoral situation. Five husbands! Is this a woman looking for love?

Looking for Love in the Wrong Place

Divorce was very common in Jesus' day. Among the Jews, husbands were putting their wives away quicker than they put away their coats, and for any cause that came to mind. It is not likely that higher standards existed for the Samaritans.

The woman does not deny Jesus' statement, but rather confesses that it is true by acknowledging Him as a prophet. She is quick to move the conversation in a different direction. After all, who wants to talk about their personal sin? Teach me, but do not tell me about my sin. She recognizes Jesus as a man of God, but she does not know that He is the Messiah.

Word Study

The Greek word for *husband* is *aner*, meaning "a man (properly as an individual male):–fellow, husband, man, sir."

John 4

[20] "Our fathers worshiped in this mountain, and you people say that in Jerusalem is the place where men ought to worship."

[21] Jesus said to her, "Woman, believe Me, an hour is coming when neither in this mountain nor in Jerusalem will you worship the Father.

[22] "You worship what you do not know; we worship what we know, for salvation is from the Jews.

[23] "But an hour is coming, and now is, when the true worshipers will worship the Father in spirit

Love Transforms

and truth; for such people the Father seeks to be His worshipers.
^{24} "God is spirit, and those who worship Him must worship in spirit and truth."

Amazing that she desires to know about worship but is willing to ignore the sin issue. She knew adultery was sin, but she'd tried marriage five times and it hadn't worked. Wanting to be loved, but wanting to avoid pain, why not try another way?

No matter which way you cut it, sin is an obstacle to blessings. It is also a major obstacle and a serious block to worshipping in spirit and in truth. Today, in the Christian community, we want to be taught deep truths; we want to work on controversial issues, but we don't deal with sin. We want to know the ins and outs of worship and praise, but choose to do whatever suits us. We compartmentalize our Christianity. We'll go to church on Sunday or read the Bible for Bible study, but do not use the Scriptures as our standard for every area of our lives.

"Yes," the Samaritan woman says, "our fathers believe this and you believe that." No mention that she is living with a man. Jesus, in His mercy and love, teaches her that the physical place of worship is not important, because the heart of worship is spiritual. God made the earth and everything in it, and He is the Lord over all. He dwells in a temple not made by human hands

Looking for Love in the Wrong Place

and is not worshipped by human hands, as though He needed anything. The heart must worship in spirit and in truth.

John 4

^{25} The woman said to Him, "I know that Messiah is coming (He who is called Christ); when that One comes, He will declare all things to us."
^{26} Jesus said to her, "I who speak to you am He."
^{27} At this point His disciples came, and they were amazed that He had been speaking with a woman, yet no one said, "What do You seek?" or, "Why do You speak with her?"

The Samaritans studied the Torah and knew that the Messiah was coming. This woman knew about the Messiah, that He was coming and that He would declare all things. She knew Jesus was a prophet, but did not realize He was the Messiah.

Christ gently disclosed to this woman more than he had told even His disciples at this point. Oh, to be talking directly with Jesus and not know who He is! *Who is this man?* She wondered. She had never seen Him before, yet He revealed her hidden past. And this man, a Jew, had asked her, a Samaritan, for a drink of water. But then He offered her living, eternal water instead.

This man, whom she recognized as a prophet, at last reveals to her, "I who speak to you am He." Unconditional love looks at a Samaritan woman, a half-breed, a sinner, with the desire to bring her to a level of wholeness, not just with accusations, but also with solutions. She is given another chance, even though she is living in sin.

When the disciples returned they were amazed that He had been talking to this woman. They didn't get it. But she did!

John 4

^{28} So the woman left her waterpot, and went into the city and said to the men,
^{29} "Come, see a man who told me all the things that I have done; this is not the Christ, is it?"
^{30} They went out of the city, and were coming to Him.

The woman left her water pot. She had come to the well to draw water, but made a complete turnaround. Living water already springing up in her, she left behind what she was doing to move forward with her newfound information, a belief that transformed her to go tell others about the Messiah. The love of God will take you further than you thought you would ever go.

It is interesting that she went to the men and not the women. Her background suggests she had a way with men. Certainly if there was a change, they would be the first to recognize it. With the outpouring of the living water, she was able to convince them to see for themselves. Without a lesson in "how to lead someone

Looking for Love in the Wrong Place

to Christ," without being told to go tell others, the woman is off to tell the story. From sinner to evangelist, the message was short: "Come see a man who told me all the things I have done."

John 4

³⁹ From that city many of the Samaritans believed in Him because of the word of the woman who testified, "He told me all the things that I have done."
⁴⁰ So when the Samaritans came to Jesus, they were asking Him to stay with them; and He stayed there two days.

As if in shock, she keeps repeating, "He told me all the things that I have done" (verses 29 and 39). The love of Christ so permeated the heart of this Samaritan woman that her message was fully believed.

There were times when the messages of the prophets were not believed (John 5:46-47). But many sought Jesus because they believed this woman's story. Longing to receive the same gift, the people streamed out toward Jesus. They must have seen a radical change in her! The people were so excited, they asked Jesus to stay with them. He and His disciples stayed for two days.

John 4

⁴¹ Many more believed because of His word;
⁴² and they were saying to the woman, "It is no longer because of what you said that we believe, for

Love Transforms

we have heard for ourselves and know that this One is indeed the Savior of the world."

At first, some believed because they had heard the woman. After they heard, they believed for themselves and knew that Jesus was indeed the world's Savior. God's love reaches beyond our expectations. The gospel had been extended to a Samaritan (not just Jews), to a woman (not just men), and beyond the racial barrier (not just a particular group). God is no respecter of persons. The gospel is available to whosoever will come.

This woman had been the wife of five different men and was living with another. Not until she found true love in Jesus and partook of the living water of life freely did her influence on men result in investments that would last throughout eternity.

Looking for Love in the Wrong Place

Selah…Think about it.

1. Read 1 John 4:19 and 5:3. How can we love God, and what is the proof of that love?

   _____

   _____

   _____

2. What hope or cure is there for immorality in 1 Corinthians 6:9-11?

   _____

   _____

   _____

3. Is there an issue of sin that you need to deal with?

   _____

   _____

   _____

4. Is it OK for two people to live together if they're not married? If you are planning to get married, can you try living together first? Can you have sex every now and then with anyone you want? Check the following Scriptures and write out your answers.

Love Transforms

Exodus 20:14

_____

_____

_____

1 Corinthians 6:9

_____

_____

_____

1 Corinthians 6:18

_____

_____

_____

Ephesians 5:3

_____

_____

_____

5. What can you do to keep from fornicating or committing adultery? Read 1 Corinthians 7:2; 1 Thessalonians 4:3-5.

_____

_____

_____

Looking for Love in the Wrong Place

6. Can you be forgiven if you have already had sex outside of marriage? Read 1 John 2:1; 1 Corinthians 6:11.

   _____

   _____

   _____

7. How would you explain to someone how to look for love that will last and the impact that love can have on his or her life and the lives of others?

   _____

   _____

   _____

8. How would you explain to someone what it means to worship "in spirit and in truth"?

   _____

   _____

   _____

Chapter 7

LOVE TRAP
CAUGHT IN ADULTERY

Early in the morning, about daybreak, Jesus was in the temple, teaching a huge crowd of people. The people were excited, some really wanting to be taught and others waiting for an opportunity to criticize and find a way to trap Jesus. Either way they were enthusiastic about hearing the Teacher again. Jesus spoke with power and authority that always amazed the crowd.

Suddenly the mood changed; the sound of muffled cries could be heard. The crowd gasped as a group of men half-dragged, half-carried a woman into their midst. Underline the accusation in the verses below.

John 8

³ The scribes and the Pharisees brought a woman caught in adultery, and having set her in the center of the court,

Looking for Love in the Wrong Place

> ⁴ they said to Him, "Teacher, this woman has been caught in adultery, in the very act.
> ⁵ "Now in the Law Moses commanded us to stone such women; what then do You say?"

Talk about looking for love in the wrong place. This woman, obviously the center of attention, cowered in embarrassment as the men spoke to Jesus. The crowd listened in amazement as the men, with coarse brutality, presented their accusation to Jesus. They cited the Law as they talked about stoning the woman they had just caught in adultery.

Death was the punishment for a married woman guilty of adultery (Lev. 20:10; Deut. 22:22). In some cases, stoning was commanded (Deut. 22:23-24) or strangulation and in Ezek. 16:40 thrusting through with a sword. The text does not tell us if she is a betrothed virgin, unmarried or married, only that she was caught in adultery. But punishing the woman wasn't the real issue here. The whole point was to catch Jesus.

Deuteronomy 22
> ²² If a man is found lying with a married woman, then both of them shall die, the man who lay with the woman, and the woman; thus you shall purge the evil from Israel.

Death, whether by stoning or strangulation or some other means, seemed imminent. The woman's accusers

Love Trap

knew what the Law said. They knew what Moses commanded. But they wanted to know what Jesus had to say.

Notice, no one even mentioned the other half of this adulterous duo. How can you catch one person in adultery and not the other? But then, these accusers had a different purpose. For them, it was not really about adultery, living holy, or purging evil from their community. It was not about the sin; it was really about Jesus.

Read the next verse, underlining the purpose for this early-morning drill.

> They were saying this, testing Him, so that they might have grounds for accusing Him. But Jesus stooped down and with His finger wrote on the ground.
> —John 8:6

The woman, obviously guilty, was "caught in the act." Talk about feeling like trash. Did she even have time to dress? Yet there she was, facing certain death.

But these men didn't care about her. They were only using her to test Jesus.

She glanced around. Running was out of the question. The situation seemed hopeless. No one seemed concerned about what happened to her. So there she stood, accused and guilty in front of all those people, with little or no clothing on. What had started as a

Looking for Love in the Wrong Place

morning of passion with a forbidden lover had turned into a public trial, no lover in sight. Or so she thought.

Jesus did not say a word. Had He even heard the question? The woman remained silent too. Best to blend in with the surroundings, melt into the background as much as a half-naked woman could, standing in the center of the synagogue.

Jesus stooped and wrote in the dirt. All eyes were on the ground, where the message was written, but they didn't get it. They pressed Jesus. The trap had been set and they were waiting for Jesus to fall into it. "What do you say, Jesus?"

John 8

7 But when they persisted in asking Him, He straightened up, and said to them, "He who is without sin among you, let him be the first to throw a stone at her."

8 Again He stooped down and wrote on the ground.

9 When they heard it, they began to go out one by one, beginning with the older ones, and He was left alone, and the woman, where she was, in the center of the court.

How quickly the tables turned. If you really want to talk about sin, we can talk about it—all of it. Jesus does not say another word, but the implication is there.

Love Trap

The law was clear regarding evildoers. There was to be a minimum of two or three witnesses. The hand of the witnesses were to be first against the offender to put him to death, and afterward the hand of all the people. The purpose was so the witnesses might feel their responsibility in giving evidence and that the evil would be purged from their midst (Deut. 17:6-7).

Jesus was putting these men to the test. Without pronouncing judgment on her case, he directed them, if any of them were innocent, to perform the office of executioner. He said this, knowing full well their guilt, and knowing that no one would dare to do it.

A hush fell over the crowd. Tension filled the air as everyone waited for the stones to fly. But the trap these men had set for Jesus had become their own.

He stooped again and wrote on the ground. What did Jesus write? We don't know. But whatever it was drove His point home.

Jesus brought the woman back into the picture. "He who is without sin among you, let him be the first to throw a stone at her." When they heard that, they all began to leave. Stones dropped, one here, one there. They did not run off, just slipped away one by one until it was just Jesus and the woman standing in the center of the court. Jesus said to her, "Woman, where are they? Did no one condemn you?"

Looking for Love in the Wrong Place

John 8

¹⁰ Straightening up, Jesus said to her, "Woman, where are they? Did no one condemn you?"

¹¹ She said, "No one, Lord." And Jesus said, "I do not condemn you, either. Go. From now on sin no more."

She knew she was guilty. Jesus knew she was guilty. By this time the entire town knew she was guilty. But Jesus said to her, "I do not condemn you, either. Go. From now on sin no more." He did not accuse her, He did not give her a sermon, and He did not throw a stone.

Word Study

The Greek word for *condemn* is *katakrino*, meaning "to judge against, i.e. sentence:–condemn, damn. To pronounce sentence against, condemn, adjudge guilty." To 'go' and 'sin' no more are both present imperatives, which means, she was commanded to go and from that point sin was not to be repeated or continued, adultery or any other sin.

Jesus knows she is guilty, but does not condemn her or judge her. He does not count her sin against her. He simply tells her to go and not continue in sin. Sounds like what happens to our sins at salvation. She started the day with one lover, but ended up with the "lover of her soul," Jesus Christ. She started out with sin, but

Love Trap

ended up with a pardon. She should have had death, but ended up with her life.

Her last words to Him were, "No one, Lord." Lord? The Greek word for "Lord" is *Kurios*. It means "master, ruler, one who controls." That is what she called Jesus.

Read Ephesians 2:4-6 and 3:17-19. Describe what happens when we become rooted and grounded in God's love.

Ephesians 2

[4] But God, being rich in mercy, because of His great love with which He loved us,

[5] even when we were dead in our transgressions, made us alive together with Christ (by grace you have been saved),

[6] and raised us up with Him, and seated us with Him in the heavenly places in Christ Jesus,

What happens?

_____

_____

_____

Ephesians 3

[17] So that Christ may dwell in your hearts through faith; and that you, being rooted and grounded in love,

Looking for Love in the Wrong Place

¹⁸ may be able to comprehend with all the saints what is the breadth and length and height and depth,
¹⁹ and to know the love of Christ which surpasses knowledge, that you may be filled up to all the fullness of God.

What happens?

_____

_____

_____

Isaiah 54

¹⁰ "For the mountains may be removed and the hills may shake, but My lovingkindness will not be removed from you, and My covenant of peace will not be shaken," says the LORD who has compassion on you.

Write out God's promise.

_____

_____

_____

No matter what happens and no matter what the circumstance, God already has a plan. He says His favor, His lovingkindness, will not be removed and His covenant will not be shaken. Can you live with that?

Love Trap

Selah…Think about it.

1. If you had a friend who was in the arms of someone who was not his or her spouse, what Scripture would you use from this lesson to encourage that person to repent? What Scripture would you give your friend to show that he or she has been forgiven?

   _____

   _____

   _____

2. Can you list at least three actions you would take (or encourage someone else to take) when situations seem overwhelming?

   _____

   _____

   _____

3. As a result of God's promise to work all things together for the good of those who love Him and are called according to His purpose (Rom. 8:28), what can you know? How should you respond in any given situation based on that knowledge?

   _____

   _____

   _____

Looking for Love in the Wrong Place

4. How should we respond to God's incredible promise that He will not remove His lovingkindness from us (Isa. 54:10)?

   _____

   _____

   _____

5. When guilt from past sins rushes into the present like a bulldozer, what Scripture will you take comfort in?

   _____

   _____

   _____

6. What are the benefits of Jesus being the lover of your soul? What was the significance of the woman calling Jesus, 'Lord'?

   _____

   _____

   _____

7. How would you explain to someone how to look for love that will last and the impact that love can have on his or her life and the lives of others?

   _____

   _____

   _____

Love Trap

8. What is love? Read 1 John 4:10 and John 3:16 and write the description given by God.

   _____

   _____

   _____

9. Definitions of the Greek words for love are listed below. How do these definitions help you understand love?

   _____

   _____

   _____

Scripture to meditate on:

Now may our Lord Jesus Christ Himself and God our Father, who has loved us and given us eternal comfort and good hope by grace, comfort and strengthen your hearts in every good work and word. (2 Thess. 2:16-17)

Word Study

There are four Greek words for love. Let's look at some definitions to help us understand the various meanings for each word. According to *Wuest's Word Studies from the Greek New Testament*:

"*Agapao* speaks of a love that is awakened by a sense of value in an object, which causes one to prize it. It

Looking for Love in the Wrong Place

springs from an apprehension of the preciousness of an object. It is a love of esteem and approbation. The quality of this love is determined by the character of the one who loves, and that of the object loved". This is the word used for God's unconditional love. It is used more than three hundred times in the New Testament.

"*Agapa*o is used in John 3:16. God's love for a sinful and lost race springs from His heart in response to the high value He places upon each human soul. Every sinner is exceedingly precious in His sight."

This love takes the initiative in the relationship regardless of what response it receives.

"*Phileo* is a love that consists of the glow of the heart kindled by the perception of that in the object which affords us pleasure. It is the response of the human spirit to what appeals to it as pleasurable. The Greeks made much of friendship. The word was used to speak of a friendly affection. It is a love called out of one in response to a feeling of pleasure or delight which one experiences from an apprehension of qualities in another that furnish such pleasure or delight."

Phileo is found in Revelation 22:15; Matthew 6:5; 10:37; 23:6; Luke 20:46; John 11:3, 36; 1 Corinthians 16:22. Both *Agapeo* and *Phileo* are used in John 21:15-17.

Phileo is a love that wants to give and receive. It responds to acts of kindness, tenderness, or appreciation. It is concerned about another's happiness as well as its own.

Love Trap

***Strong's Concordance* combines *Phileo* and *Storge*:**

Philostorgos refers to "cherishing one's kindred, especially parents or children. The Authorized Version translates it once as "kindly affectioned." The word also means the mutual love of parents and children and wives and husbands. It includes loving affection, prone to love, loving tenderly; chiefly of the reciprocal tenderness of parents and children."

Storge refers to "a natural affection or obligation. Its basis is one's own nature. It is the natural affection that wells up within for your spouse and your child. It can come and go." It is used in the New Testament only in the negative, as *astorge*. (See 2 Tim. 3:3 and Rom. 12:10.)

Eros is the only Greek word for love that is not found in the Bible. It refers to a passion that seizes and overmasters the mind. This type of love dominates our culture. It is self-centered and when it gives, it looks for what it can receive. *Webster* defines it as "a sexual love, an erotic love or desire."

Chapter 8

FOR THE LOVE OF MONEY
ANANIAS AND SAPPHIRA

Sapphira lived during an exciting time in church history. Times were certainly changing! Her ancestors had longed for and looked forward to this time. The promise of the Holy Spirit had been fulfilled. It happened on the Day of Pentecost.

Jerusalem was crowded with devout men from every nation. The disciples were gathered together in one place, and when they began to speak of the mighty deeds of God, everyone could hear and understand them in his or her own language. The crowd thought the disciples were drunk until Peter spoke up. He told them what they were experiencing had been prophesied by the prophet Joel. He talked to them about Jesus and the miracles, signs, and wonders God had performed through Him. He told them of God's predetermined plan and the part

Looking for Love in the Wrong Place

they had played in it by nailing Jesus to the cross and putting Him to death. He told the crowd that God had raised Jesus from the dead since it was impossible for Him to be held by the power of death. He told them that Jesus had been exalted to the right hand of God and He had poured forth the Holy Spirit that they were experiencing (Acts 2).

The people were encouraged to repent, be baptized, and receive the gift of the Holy Spirit. Peter solemnly exhorted them to be saved. The response was overwhelming; about three thousand people received and believed the Word that day.

Yes, Sapphira lived in exciting times. The coming of the Holy Spirit and the beginning of the church of Jesus Christ all occurred during her lifetime.

Read the following verses, noting how the people responded after they believed. Underline the points.

Acts 2

42 They were continually devoting themselves to the apostles' teaching and to fellowship, to the breaking of bread and to prayer.

43 Everyone kept feeling a sense of awe; and many wonders and signs were taking place through the apostles.

44 And all those who had believed were together and had all things in common;

For the Love of Money

^{45} and they began selling their property and possessions and were sharing them with all, as anyone might have need.

Response to the Word:

_____

_____

_____

The people were eating together, studying together, praying together, and they all had a sense of awe. They sold their property and provided for those who had a need. Read the last two verses in Acts 2, underlining the heart response and what God was doing with the number in this church.

Acts 2

^{46} Day by day continuing with one mind in the temple, and breaking bread from house to house, they were taking their meals together with gladness and sincerity of heart,

^{47} praising God and having favor with all the people. And the Lord was adding to their number day by day those who were being saved.

Although the early church had single-minded devotion, they met with much opposition. But the apostles understood their God-given authority; they exercised it

Looking for Love in the Wrong Place

and they walked in it. They preached the uncompromising gospel with boldness; they healed the lame and were recognized as having been with Jesus.

The authorities (chief priests and elders) threw them into prison for their actions. Undaunted, the apostles prayed with such fervor that the whole place was shaken and they spoke the Word with boldness. Read the following verse underlining how the congregation is described.

Acts 4

[32] And the congregation of those who believed were of one heart and soul; and not one of them claimed that anything belonging to him was his own, but all things were common property to them.

The early church continued with one heart and soul, meeting the needs of everyone in the congregation. The apostles were constantly teaching the gospel and the abundant grace of Jesus was upon them all. Properties were sold; the proceeds were given to the apostles, who in turn made distribution to those who had need.

Sapphira and her husband, Ananias, were part of this congregation, the fastest-growing church in the world, where about five thousand men had heard the message and believed. It was in this congregation and during this time that Ananias and Sapphira sold a piece of property. Read Acts 5:1-2, underlining the action taken after the property was sold.

For the Love of Money

Acts 5

¹ But a man named Ananias, with his wife Sapphira, sold a piece of property,
² and kept back some of the price for himself, with his wife's full knowledge, and bringing a portion of it, he laid it at the apostles' feet.

The reason various members of the congregation were selling their property was simply to provide for those who had need within the congregation. Even Barnabas, who owned a tract of land, sold it and laid the proceeds at the apostles' feet (Acts 4:36-37). Ananias sharply contrasted with Barnabas by bringing only a portion of the proceeds. (The word *but* at the beginning of Acts 5:1 represents a contrast to the previous verses.)

The rules for selling property and bringing proceeds were fairly simple. The donor must: (a) be a member of the congregation, (b) own the property, (c) voluntarily sell the property, and (d) voluntarily contribute the proceeds. But Ananias (the name means "God is gracious") and Sapphira agreed to keep back some of the proceeds. That would have been OK except they said the amount given was the full selling price.

Read and underline Peter's questions in verses 3-4. Circle *God* and the *Holy Spirit* and mark *lie* or *lied.*

Acts 5

³ But Peter said, "Ananias, why has Satan filled your heart to lie to the Holy Spirit and to keep back some of the price of the land?

Looking for Love in the Wrong Place

⁴ "While it remained unsold, did it not remain your own? And after it was sold, was it not under your control? Why is it that you have conceived this deed in your heart? You have not lied to men but to God."

Keep in mind that this couple professed Christianity, believing in Jesus and receiving forgiveness of their sins. They had repented, been baptized, and devoted themselves to the apostles' teaching, to fellowship and to the breaking of bread. They were very much a part of the early church and all it stood for.

It is very interesting that they were a part of a faith group. What you see is not always what you get. They agreed together to say that the donated amount of their property was the full selling price. Peter, getting to the heart of the matter, reminded Ananias that the property was his to do with as he desired and challenged him on the lie.

Did you notice whom Peter said he lied to? If not, read verses 3 and 4 again and record your answer.

Ananias lied to:

_____

_____

_____

For the Love of Money

Read verses 5 and 6, underlining what happened to Ananias.

Acts 5

⁵ And as he heard these words, Ananias fell down and breathed his last; and great fear came over all who heard of it.
⁶ The young men got up and covered him up, and after carrying him out, they buried him.

Ananias's lie brought him death, and fear came upon those who heard about it. There had been such an outpouring of the Holy Spirit, Peter's concern was not that Ananias had lied to him or to the church, but that he lied to the *Holy Spirit* (vs. 3), also called *God* in verse 4.

Why the lie? Could it have been to get attention, to be (or at least to look) like everyone else in the church? Perhaps it was to get the same recognition that Barnabas received. (Remember the contrasted verse in Acts 5:1?) Driven by the desire for prestige, position, power, or some other poorly motivated reason for giving, their initial act of generosity turned sour.

Peter made it clear that the couple was in control of their property before and after the sale, so the money was theirs to do with as they chose. So the major issue for Peter was not the money, but the lie. Read the following verses, recording what God says about lies and liars.

Looking for Love in the Wrong Place

Psalms 63

¹¹ But the king will rejoice in God; everyone who swears by Him will glory, for the mouths of those who speak lies will be stopped.

___

___

___

Proverbs 19

⁵ A false witness will not go unpunished, and he who tells lies will not escape.
⁹ A false witness will not go unpunished, and he who tells lies will perish.

Don't miss the difference in verses 5 and 9.

___

___

___

Isaiah 44

²⁴ Thus saith the LORD, thy redeemer, and he that formed thee from the womb, I am the LORD that maketh all things; that stretcheth forth the heavens alone; that spreadeth abroad the earth by myself;

For the Love of Money

²⁵ That frustrateth the tokens of the liars, and maketh diviners mad; that turneth wise men backward, and maketh their knowledge foolish (KJV)

_____

_____

_____

One more verse on liars. Circle the word *liars* and record your findings.

Revelation 21

⁸ But for the cowardly and unbelieving and abominable and murderers and immoral persons and sorcerers and idolaters and all liars, their part will be in the lake that burns with fire and brimstone, which is the second death.

_____

_____

_____

Is there an antidote, a cure for lying? Of course. It is Jesus, who says, "I am the way, and the *truth*, and the life" (John 14:6, emphasis added). In John 17:17, Jesus said, "Your Word is truth." Jesus also said, "and you will know the *truth* and the *truth* will make you *free*" (John 8:32, emphasis added).

Looking for Love in the Wrong Place

Word Study

The Greek word for *make* and *free* is *eleutheroo* (el-yoo-ther-o'-o), meaning "to liberate, i.e. (figuratively) to exempt (from moral, ceremonial or mortal liability):-deliver, make free."

This account of Ananias and Sapphira makes it clear that there is no halfway mark with truth; something is either a lie or it is truth. Obviously financially able to provide help to others in this new church community, Ananias and Sapphira had a great opportunity to bless and be blessed. Instead they pretended to be something they were not. In the eyes of the people they appeared generous, but in the eyes of God they were hypocrites.

What about the money issue? Their lie was tied to a concern for the money, a love for money. We talk about it; we sing about it; we think about it daily; we long for it; we work for it; we *need* it. We use it to provide for our families, and yet it has broken up families. Many have killed for it, died for it, lived for it; some have gone to jail for it. It can be a source of dissension or a source of reward.

Whether it is too much money or not enough, unforeseen economic difficulties, poor financial management, or unbearable financial pressures in a world that appears to be in chaos, it could be a problem if not properly managed. What does the Bible say about managing money, about financial freedom and financial wisdom?

For the Love of Money

Did you know that about half of the parables in the Bible address money and finances? The decisions we make concerning money will affect every area of our lives. It certainly affected the lives of Ananias and Sapphira! God cannot be separated from the subject. If you really want financial freedom and financial wisdom, follow God's principles.

Read the following passage and record any principles you find.

1 Timothy 6

⁹ But those who want to get rich fall into temptation and a snare and many foolish and harmful desires which plunge men into ruin and destruction.
¹⁰ For the love of money is a root of all sorts of evil, and some by longing for it have wandered away from the faith and pierced themselves with many griefs.
¹¹ But flee from these things, you man of God, and pursue righteousness, godliness, faith, love, perseverance and gentleness.
¹² Fight the good fight of faith; take hold of the eternal life to which you were called, and you made the good confession in the presence of many witnesses.

The principles:

_____

_____

_____

Looking for Love in the Wrong Place

Timothy is described as a "man of God" in verse 11, and he is told to flee and to pursue. In verse 12, he is told to fight the good fight of faith. Have you ever considered good stewardship a part of fighting the good fight?

Proverbs 15

^{27} He who profits illicitly troubles his own house, but he who hates bribes will live.

The principle:

___

___

___

Luke 12

^{15} Then He said to them, "Beware, and be on your guard against every form of greed; for not even when one has an abundance does his life consist of his possessions."

The principle:

___

___

___

For the Love of Money

Ecclesiastes 5

¹⁰ He who loves money will not be satisfied with money, nor he who loves abundance with its income. This too is vanity.

The principle:

_____

_____

_____

Remember, God owns it all. He didn't create the earth and then turn it over to man. He retained ownership. Our assignment is to manage it and to be good stewards of God's property (Ps. 24:1-2). The one who is faithful with little will be faithful with much. The one who is unrighteous in little is unrighteous in much (Luke 16:11-13). In other words, if you cannot properly manage three dollars, why would God provide more?

Before God can financially bless us, we have to prove to be good managers of what He has already provided. We are clearly told that if we sow sparingly, we will reap sparingly; if we sow bountifully, we will reap bountifully. We are not to give grudgingly or under compulsion, but as we purpose in our hearts. God is looking for cheerful givers. He has promised not only to supply seed to the sower, but also to multiply the seed and provide an increase in righteousness (2 Cor. 9:6-10). Read 1

Looking for Love in the Wrong Place

Timothy 6:17 and record the principles. Look for more than one!

> **1 Timothy 6**
>
> ¹⁷ Instruct those who are rich in this present world not to be conceited or to fix their hope on the uncertainty of riches, but on God, who richly supplies us with all things to enjoy.

The principles:

_____

_____

_____

Looking for love in the wrong place, whether of an object or a person, can only lead to destruction. God tells us not to fix our hope on the uncertainty of riches. He is the one who supplies us with all things to enjoy. He gives power to make wealth (Deut. 8:18). He owns it all and supplies it all. He provides the energy, strength, personality, wisdom, knowledge, understanding, and skills to earn wealth.

Unfortunately Ananias had his hope fixed on something other than God and he lost it all. His wife, not knowing what had happened to her husband, came in three hours later, and she lost it all too.

Read Acts 5:8-9, underlining Peter's questions. Circle *price*, *agreed*, and *Spirit of the Lord*.

For the Love of Money

Acts 5

⁸ And Peter responded to her, "Tell me whether you sold the land for such and such a price?" And she said, "Yes, that was the price."
⁹ Then Peter said to her, "Why is it that you have agreed together to put the Spirit of the Lord to the test? Behold, the feet of those who have buried your husband are at the door, and they will carry you out as well."

This situation turns out to be a lot more serious than Ananias or Sapphira ever imagined. We too are often unaware of the seriousness of our relationship with Jesus and the need to walk in obedience to Him who works in us to will and to do of His good pleasure.

The opportunity was provided for Sapphira (her name means "beautiful") to tell the truth, but she held on to the statement she and her husband had decided upon. Submission to her husband was not the issue, nor was it submission to Peter or to the church. Peter's concern was that she had lied to the Holy Spirit based on an agreement with her husband, whom she put above God.

In this same chapter (5:29) Peter and John say to the council and the high priest, "We must obey God rather than men." The effect on the early church was immediate and unbelievably overwhelming. Read Acts 5:10, underlining what happened to Sapphira and circling the impact on the church.

Looking for Love in the Wrong Place

Acts 5

¹⁰ And immediately she fell at his feet and breathed her last, and the young men came in and found her dead, and they carried her out and buried her beside her husband.

¹¹ And great fear came over the whole church, and over all who heard of these things.

Ananias and Sapphira, looking for love in the wrong place, lied and died. The new church was purged, and the believers stood in awe of God and of the result of sin. The early church grew, and multitudes of men and women were constantly added to their number.

What would the church look like today if God's judgment were as swift now as it was then? Liars will be judged but lies can be forgiven, as with any other sin. Money cannot buy the favor of God, but obedience brings honor and the blessings of God.

For the Love of Money

Selah…Think about it.

1. Why is the love of money the root of all evil? (1 Tim. 6:10) Understanding that you cannot serve God and money (Matt. 6:24), is your hope fixed on money or God? Really? What's your proof?

   _____

   _____

   _____

2. What is God's solution for lying? What encouragement would you give to a habitual liar?

   _____

   _____

   _____

3. Will God hold a woman responsible if she submits to her husband even though the submission is in opposition to the Word of God? How would you support your answer with Scripture?

   _____

   _____

   _____

4. Was Peter too hard on Ananias and Sapphira? Was Peter responsible for their deaths?

   _____

Looking for Love in the Wrong Place

_____

_____

5. What purpose did their deaths serve? Why was there great fear on the whole church?

_____

_____

_____

6. Evaluate your reasons for giving. If your motivation is based on your love for Jesus, does your checkbook show it?

_____

_____

_____

7. Read the list below, considering the things that money will not buy. What other items would you add to the list?

_____

_____

_____

For the Love of Money

Money will buy:
A bed but not sleep.
Books but not brains.
Food but not appetite.
Finery but not beauty.
A house but not a home.
Medicine but not health.
Luxuries but not culture.
A crucifix but not a Savior.
A church pew but not heaven.
Amusement but not happiness.

Chapter 9

BUSHELS OF LOVE
RUTH AND BOAZ, THE KINSMAN REDEEMER

A light, though just a glimmer, is seen during the time of the judges. The word of the Lord was rare during that dark period in the life of the nation of Israel. This love story illustrates the responsibility of man and the sovereignty of God in the lives of His people. God orchestrates the events, as Ruth, who is in distress and in need, meets Boaz, who becomes her kinsman redeemer, willing to love and protect her. He was a willing and able redeemer that radically changed her life. The light in this magnificent story of Ruth and Boaz is a surprising contrast to a time when everyone was doing what was right in his or her own eyes. Look for the story behind the story that can radically change your life!

Ruth, a Moabite woman, was married to an Israelite man named Mahlon. Mahlon had journeyed to Moab

Looking for Love in the Wrong Place

with his parents and his brother because there was a famine in the land of Judah. Moab, land of fertile and well-watered highlands, was east of the Dead Sea. After Mahlon's father, Elimelech, died, his sons married and lived in Moab for about ten years. Then the boys died, leaving their mother, Naomi, and their wives.

Naomi heard there was food once again in Judah and decided to return to her homeland. The trip to Judah, about 120 miles, would be a long and dangerous journey through desolate places, especially for three women with little or no money and no visible protection. Both daughters-in-law started out with her, but only Ruth continued. Read the following verses to determine Naomi's relationship with her daughters-in-law.

Ruth 1

8 And Naomi said to her two daughters-in-law, "Go, return each of you to her mother's house. May the LORD deal kindly with you as you have dealt with the dead and with me.

9 "May the LORD grant that you may find rest, each in the house of her husband." Then she kissed them, and they lifted up their voices and wept.

10 And they said to her, "No, but we will surely return with you to your people."

11 But Naomi said, "Return, my daughters. Why should you go with me? Have I yet sons in my womb, that they may be your husbands?

Bushels of Love

¹² "Return, my daughters! Go, for I am too old to have a husband. If I said I have hope, if I should even have a husband tonight and also bear sons,

¹³ "would you therefore wait until they were grown? Would you therefore refrain from marrying? No, my daughters; for it is harder for me than for you, for the hand of the LORD has gone forth against me."

¹⁴ And they lifted up their voices and wept again; and Orpah kissed her mother-in-law, but Ruth clung to her.

Naomi had a great relationship with her daughters-in-law and wanted the best for them. She wanted them to be married. Orpah returned to Moab, but Ruth remained with Naomi. Go back and read verse 13. What does Naomi say about the Lord? Naomi continues to encourage Ruth to return. Read the next passage to see why Ruth refuses.

Ruth 1

¹⁵ Then she said, "Behold, your sister-in-law has gone back to her people and her gods; return after your sister-in-law."

¹⁶ But Ruth said, "Do not urge me to leave you or turn back from following you; for where you go, I will go, and where you lodge, I will lodge. Your people shall be my people, and your God, my God.

¹⁷ "Where you die, I will die, and there I will be buried. Thus may the LORD do to me, and worse, if anything but death parts you and me."

Looking for Love in the Wrong Place

¹⁸ When she saw that she was determined to go with her, she said no more to her.

Obviously Naomi had said or done something in her walk to cause such a wonderful response to erupt from Ruth. She was willing to leave all she had (her country, her relatives, and the opportunity to remarry in her own country) to follow her mother-in-law and to worship the God of Naomi.

It is interesting that mothers-in-law today are often talked about as being absolutely dreadful. This is a story to be told in every family!

Naomi is so distraught, her own people barely recognize her. She asks them not to even call her Naomi, which means "pleasant," but to call her Mara, which means "bitter." Read the following verses and underline why she is so bitter.

Ruth 1

²⁰ She said to them, "Do not call me Naomi; call me Mara, for the Almighty has dealt very bitterly with me.
²¹ "I went out full, but the LORD has brought me back empty. Why do you call me Naomi, since the LORD has witnessed against me and the Almighty has afflicted me?"

Like many who are caught up in the problems and circumstances of life, Naomi blamed God for her

Bushels of Love

emptiness, and she believed God had witnessed against her. Everyone was aware that she had lost her husband, her sons, and the property they had taken with them.

Although bitter, Naomi acknowledged the power of God and gave no credit to Satan. She also realized God was the One who had brought her back. Although she felt empty, God had a tremendous plan for her.

It was the time of barley harvest, and Ruth was anxious to go out to glean or gather what the harvesters had left behind. She was willing to work in the field of anyone with whom she found favor so the two of them could have food. Naomi encouraged her to go.

Ruth happened to come to the field of Boaz, an extremely wealthy man. Boaz noticed her right away and wanted to know who she was. His workmen knew all about her: She was a Moabite woman, she was with Naomi, and she was a hard worker. In a small town, everybody knows everybody's business!

Read the following verses, underlining what Boaz said to Ruth.

Ruth 2

8 Then Boaz said to Ruth, "Listen carefully, my daughter. Do not go to glean in another field; furthermore, do not go on from this one, but stay here with my maids.

9 "Let your eyes be on the field which they reap, and go after them. Indeed, I have commanded the

Looking for Love in the Wrong Place

servants not to touch you. When you are thirsty, go to the water jars and drink from what the servants draw."

Right away Ruth obtained favor with Boaz. He offered his kindness and protection to this stranger and foreigner who was new to the area. Boaz told Ruth not to go to another field but to continue to work in his field. Perhaps this was because of the times, when great evil was going on in the nation of Israel.

Ruth was stunned and fell on her face, bowing to the ground. She said, "Why have I found favor in your sight that you should take notice of me, since I am a foreigner?" She had told Naomi she would glean in the field where she found favor, and now she is surprised at so much favor. Don't be surprised when you get what you ask for!

Read the following verses to see Boaz's reason for providing favor.

Ruth 2

[11] Boaz replied to her, "All that you have done for your mother-in-law after the death of your husband has been fully reported to me, and how you left your father and your mother and the land of your birth, and came to a people that you did not previously know.

Bushels of Love

¹² "May the LORD reward your work, and your wages be full from the LORD, the God of Israel, under whose wings you have come to seek refuge." ¹³ Then she said, "I have found favor in your sight, my lord, for you have comforted me and indeed have spoken kindly to your maidservant, though I am not like one of your maidservants."

Boaz had certainly done his homework, checking her out thoroughly. Go back and read verse 12, double underlining the blessing. He seemed to recognize that she had already taken refuge in God. Boaz pronounced a blessing upon her for her work.

Ruth had experienced plenty of hardship, and she could have become a bitter young widow. Instead she took refuge in God. She had left country and relatives and had lost her husband, but she was not self-pitying, nor was she consumed by sorrow. She is seen as meek, courteous, loyal, responsible, decisive, and modest. God was her refuge and strength.

Boaz extended special attention to Ruth at mealtime and gave specific instructions to his servants concerning her. Read these verses, looking for who served her and what the instructions were to the servants.

Ruth 2

¹⁴ At mealtime Boaz said to her, "Come here, that you may eat of the bread and dip your piece of bread in the vinegar." So she sat beside the reapers; and he

Looking for Love in the Wrong Place

served her roasted grain, and she ate and was satisfied and had some left.

¹⁵ When she rose to glean, Boaz commanded his servants, saying, "Let her glean even among the sheaves, and do not insult her.

¹⁶ "Also you shall purposely pull out for her some grain from the bundles and leave it that she may glean, and do not rebuke her."

List at least three instructions given to the servants:

1.

2.

3.

Bushels of Love

Ruth was a hard worker, and by the end of the day she had about an ephah of barley. Naomi was excited when she saw all that Ruth had gleaned and asked where she had gleaned, saying, "May he who took notice of you be blessed." When Ruth told her the field belonged to Boaz, Naomi replied, "The man is our relative, he is one of our closest relatives" (Ruth 2:19-20). Naomi, concerned about Ruth's safety, encouraged her to stay with Boaz's maids until the end of the barley and wheat harvests, about four months.

When the harvest ended Naomi came up with a brilliant idea. She still desired for Ruth to be married (Ruth 1:12-13) and she proceeded to tell her daughter-in-law how this could happen with Boaz, who was not only a close relative but also qualified to redeem her.

Read the following verses and underline Naomi's instructions to Ruth.

Ruth 3

3 "Wash yourself therefore, and anoint yourself and put on your best clothes, and go down to the threshing floor; but do not make yourself known to the man until he has finished eating and drinking.
4 "It shall be when he lies down, that you shall notice the place where he lies, and you shall go and uncover his feet and lie down; then he will tell you what you shall do."

Looking for Love in the Wrong Place

Naomi's instructions were clear, and Ruth was careful to do exactly what she was told to do.

The time for winnowing the barley was followed by a feast of celebration. After all the eating and drinking, Boaz went onto the threshing floor to lie down. Ruth went in also, uncovered his feet, and lay down. Perhaps it was the custom of the day, but Ruth was being obedient to her mother-in-law.

Boaz woke up in the middle of the night and found a woman at his feet. He did not know who she was until she said, "I am Ruth, your maid. So spread your covering over your maid, for you are a close relative." (Ruth 3:9) Needless to say, Boaz was shocked, but he was not without words to bless her. He wanted to redeem her, but there was a closer relative.

Mark the words *blessed, relative,* and *redeem. Underline* what the people in the city knew about Ruth.

Ruth 3

[10] Then he said, "May you be blessed of the LORD, my daughter. You have shown your last kindness to be better than the first by not going after young men, whether poor or rich.

[11] "Now, my daughter, do not fear. I will do for you whatever you ask, for all my people in the city know that you are a woman of excellence.

[12] "Now it is true I am a close relative; however, there is a relative closer than I.

Bushels of Love

13 "Remain this night, and when morning comes, if he will redeem you, good; let him redeem you. But if he does not wish to redeem you, then I will redeem you, as the LORD lives. Lie down until morning."

What a reputation she had built up in the short time she had been in the city! He blessed her for not going after just any man. She seemed more interested in obeying her mother-in-law to obtain a redeemer who would carry on the name of her deceased husband.

The people knew she was a woman of excellence. And Boaz was a man of integrity, admitting that he was a close relative, but there was one closer than he. He made a tentative plan. Boaz blessed her as a father, encouraged her as a woman of excellence, and promised her that a kinsman would redeem her.

Read Leviticus 25:25, 48, 49 for the law of the redeemer. Underline the requirements of the redeemer.

Leviticus 25

25 If a fellow countryman of yours becomes so poor he has to sell part of his property, then his nearest kinsman is to come and buy back what his relative has sold.

48 Then he shall have redemption right after he has been sold. One of his brothers may redeem him,

49 or his uncle, or his uncle's son, may redeem him, or one of his blood relatives from his family may redeem him; or if he prospers, he may redeem himself.

Looking for Love in the Wrong Place

The redeemer must:
- be a blood relative.
- be financially able to redeem.

Boaz was financially able to redeem the land, and he was a blood relative, but he was not the closest, and first choice had to go to the nearest kinsman.

Read Deuteronomy 25:5-10 for additional requirements for the redeemer. Underline as you read.

Deuteronomy 25

5 "When brothers live together and one of them dies and has no son, the wife of the deceased shall not be married outside the family to a strange man. Her husband's brother shall go in to her and take her to himself as wife and perform the duty of a husband's brother to her.

6 "It shall be that the firstborn whom she bears shall assume the name of his dead brother, so that his name will not be blotted out from Israel.

7 "But if the man does not desire to take his brother's wife, then his brother's wife shall go up to the gate to the elders and say, 'My husband's brother refuses to establish a name for his brother in Israel; he is not willing to perform the duty of a husband's brother to me.'

8 "Then the elders of his city shall summon him and speak to him. And if he persists and says, 'I do not desire to take her,'

Bushels of Love

⁹ then his brother's wife shall come to him in the sight of the elders, and pull his sandal off his foot and spit in his face; and she shall declare, 'Thus it is done to the man who does not build up his brother's house.'

¹⁰ "In Israel his name shall be called, 'The house of him whose sandal is removed.'"

The redeemer must:

- be a blood relative.
- have the desire to redeem.
- be willing to redeem.

Boaz was careful to protect his reputation and hers and instructed her not to leave until morning, rising before anyone could know. Ruth returned to her mother-in-law with a cloak full of food and promises of good news to come. Naomi advised her to wait and see how things would go. She believed Boaz would take care of the situation. And he did. Read on to see how Boaz resolved the problem. Mark the words *redeem* and *relative*.

Ruth 4

¹ Now Boaz went up to the gate and sat down there, and behold, the close relative of whom Boaz spoke was passing by, so he said, "Turn aside, friend, sit down here." And he turned aside and sat down.

Looking for Love in the Wrong Place

² He took ten men of the elders of the city and said, "Sit down here." So they sat down.

³ Then he said to the closest relative, "Naomi, who has come back from the land of Moab, has to sell the piece of land which belonged to our brother Elimelech.

⁴ "So I thought to inform you, saying, 'Buy it before those who are sitting here, and before the elders of my people. If you will redeem it, redeem it; but if not, tell me that I may know; for there is no one but you to redeem it, and I am after you.'" And he said, "I will redeem it."

⁵ Then Boaz said, "On the day you buy the field from the hand of Naomi, you must also acquire Ruth the Moabitess, the widow of the deceased, in order to raise up the name of the deceased on his inheritance."

⁶ The closest relative said, "I cannot redeem it for myself, because I would jeopardize my own inheritance. Redeem it for yourself; you may have my right of redemption, for I cannot redeem it."

Boaz wasted no time getting to the gate or approaching the closest relative. He had all the pieces in place. He was at the gate, he had the elders as witnesses, then he made his offer in front of all those who were present. Upon first hearing of the land, the nearest relative had the ability and the desire to purchase the land. His immediate response was, "I will redeem it."

Bushels of Love

The levirate transaction not only provided for the preservation of property, but also the welfare of widows and the continuation of family. So Boaz proceeded in his negotiation, indicating that Ruth, the widow, came with the land and the name of her husband must be raised on his inheritance. At this point the man began to relent. He said, "I cannot redeem it for myself, because I would jeopardize my own inheritance." He was a blood relative, had the ability and the desire, but when he heard all the conditions, he was not willing. He knew that if he and Ruth had children, they would be the heirs to all his fortune and he could not give an inheritance to his own family name. By preserving one name he would lose his own.

He gave his right of redemption to Boaz, who bought the land and married Ruth. Everyone was excited! Read on to see the blessings.

Ruth 4

11 All the people who were in the court, and the elders, said, "We are witnesses. May the LORD make the woman who is coming into your home like Rachel and Leah, both of whom built the house of Israel; and may you achieve wealth in Ephrathah and become famous in Bethlehem.

12 "Moreover, may your house be like the house of Perez whom Tamar bore to Judah, through the offspring which the LORD will give you by this young woman."

Looking for Love in the Wrong Place

Ruth was in good company with Rachel and Leah, who bore sons making up the twelve tribes of Israel, and Tamar, who brought forth the offspring of Judah. This young Moabite woman had married the bachelor of the century. A godly man, a man of valor and integrity, kind, willing to carry on her husband's name, and wealthy to boot. Moreover, this kinsman redeemer was from the tribe of Judah.

Read Naomi's blessing and underline the blessings.

Ruth 4

[14] Then the women said to Naomi, "Blessed is the LORD who has not left you without a redeemer today, and may his name become famous in Israel.
[15] "May he also be to you a restorer of life and a sustainer of your old age; for your daughter-in-law, who loves you and is better to you than seven sons, has given birth to him."

What a wonderful love story! I have to wonder what Boaz's mother thought of all this. His mother was Rahab the harlot, rescued from Jericho (Josh. 2, 6). She married a man named Salmon, and together they had Boaz.

Ruth and Boaz had a son named Obed, who had a son named Jesse, who had a son named David, through whom our Lord, Jesus the Christ, came. He is our kinsman redeemer, who met and fulfilled every requirement to be the redeemer.

Bushels of Love

Why did man need to be redeemed? The Bible is clear that all have sinned and come short of the glory of God (Rom. 3:10), and that not a single person is righteous; no, not one (3:23). The wages or payment for sin is death. (6:23).

Man was dead in trespasses and sins, walking according to the prince of the power of the air, indulging the desires of the flesh and of the mind (Eph. 2:1-5). We were helpless, sinners, enemies of God, and completely without hope (Rom. 5:6-10). Enslaved to sin (John 8:34), we needed a redeemer, someone without sin, to redeem us from the bondage of sin. God knew exactly what we needed. He sent His Son, Jesus!

1. He was a blood relative. Jesus came in the likeness of sinful flesh. Underline the point.

Romans 8

3 For what the Law could not do, weak as it was through the flesh, God did: sending His own Son in the likeness of sinful flesh and as an offering for sin, He condemned sin in the flesh,

4 so that the requirement of the Law might be fulfilled in us, who do not walk according to the flesh but according to the Spirit.

Here it is again in Hebrews 2. Underline the point.

Looking for Love in the Wrong Place

Hebrews 2

[14] Therefore, since the children share in flesh and blood, He Himself likewise also partook of the same, that through death He might render powerless him who had the power of death, that is, the devil,

The children share in flesh and blood, He partook of the same. Jesus became our blood relative.

2. He had the ability to pay. The kinsman redeemer had to have the means to redeem his blood relative; otherwise, the person would remain a slave. Underline the point.

2 Corinthians 5

[21] He made Him who knew no sin to be sin on our behalf, so that we might become the righteousness of God in Him.

Our redeemer had to be someone who was not enslaved to sin. Jesus did not know sin, but He was made sin on our behalf so we could be made righteous.

Here it is again in 1 Peter 1:18-19. Underline the point.

Bushels of Love

1 Peter 1

¹⁸ ...knowing that you were not redeemed with perishable things like silver or gold from your futile way of life inherited from your forefathers,
¹⁹ but with precious blood, as of a lamb unblemished and spotless, the blood of Christ.

Word Study

The Greek word for *redeem* is *lutroo*, meaning "to ransom (literally or figuratively):–redeem, to release on receipt of ransom."

Our redemption was purchased with the blood of Jesus. He was without sin (not in bondage), and He was spotless and unblemished. His work was a complete work.

With redemption came more benefits. Underline the point.

Colossians 1

¹³ For He rescued us from the domain of darkness, and transferred us to the kingdom of His beloved Son,
¹⁴ in whom we have redemption, the forgiveness of sins.

We are redeemed, rescued, transferred, and forgiven. Wonderful, isn't it? But that's not all!

Looking for Love in the Wrong Place

3. He had the desire to redeem us. Underline the point.

John 15

¹³ Greater love has no one than this, that one lay down his life for his friends.

Here it is again. Underline the point.

Luke 19

¹⁰ For the Son of Man has come to seek and to save that which was lost.

We are reminded in Hebrews 10 that the blood of bulls and goats could not take away sins, yet God required a sacrifice, and Jesus' body was prepared for that sacrifice. God took no pleasure in the animal sacrifices for the atonement of sin, but Jesus said, "Behold I have come to do Thy will, O God."(Heb. 10:7)

In Isaiah 53:10, we read that God was well pleased, satisfied. Jesus had become the propitiation (satisfaction) for our sins. He had the desire to redeem us!

4. He was willing to redeem us. He did not regard equality with God a thing to be held on to. He emptied himself. Underline the point.

Bushels of Love

Philippians 2

⁶ ...who, although He existed in the form of God, did not regard equality with God a thing to be grasped,
⁷ but emptied Himself, taking the form of a bond-servant, and being made in the likeness of men.
⁸ Being found in appearance as a man, He humbled Himself by becoming obedient to the point of death, even death on a cross.

Philippians 2:7 indicates that He took on the form of a bondservant (or a blood relative).

In Matthew 26, when Jesus was in the Garden of Gethsemane with His disciples, praying to God that if possible He would let the cup pass, the disciples could not keep their eyes open. When Jesus received the answer, He urged the men to get going. Judas went up to Jesus and kissed Him as a sign of identification to the high priest. Rambunctious Peter came to Jesus' rescue, drawing his sword and cutting off the ear of the high priest's servant.

Read the following passage, looking for Jesus' willingness to redeem us. Underline the point.

Matthew 26

⁵² Then Jesus said to him, "Put your sword back into its place; for all those who take up the sword shall perish by the sword.

Looking for Love in the Wrong Place

⁵³ "Or do you think that I cannot appeal to My Father, and He will at once put at My disposal more than twelve legions of angels?
⁵⁴ "How then will the Scriptures be fulfilled, which say that it must happen this way?"
⁵⁵ At that time Jesus said to the crowds, "Have you come out with swords and clubs to arrest Me as you would against a robber? Every day I used to sit in the temple teaching and you did not seize Me.
⁵⁶ "But all this has taken place to fulfill the Scriptures of the prophets." Then all the disciples left Him and fled.

Peter was rebuked, Judas was called friend, and the arresting party was chastised. Peter's action did not line up with the Word of God. Peter was told to put his sword away, the man's ear was healed, and the Scriptures were fulfilled.

Jesus was willing! Here it is again. Underline the point.

Hebrews 12

² ...fixing our eyes on Jesus, the author and perfecter of faith, who for the joy set before Him endured the cross, despising the shame, and has sat down at the right hand of the throne of God.
³ For consider Him who has endured such hostility by sinners against Himself, so that you will not grow weary and lose heart.

Bushels of Love

He endured the hostility of sinners, but for the joy set before Him, He endured the cross, despising the shame, and sat down at the right hand of God. He was willing!

5. Jesus also served as executioner of the murderer. Numbers 35 describes the actions of a person who unintentionally puts another to death and the cities of refuge that were set up for this purpose. It also describes what was to happen when a person was murdered intentionally and the responsibility of the blood avenger or kinsman redeemer. Read the following verses, marking the words *blood avenger* and *murderer*.

Numbers 35

19 The blood avenger himself shall put the murderer to death; he shall put him to death when he meets him.

30 If anyone kills a person, the murderer shall be put to death at the evidence of witnesses, but no person shall be put to death on the testimony of one witness.

31 Moreover, you shall not take ransom for the life of a murderer who is guilty of death, but he shall surely be put to death.

33 So you shall not pollute the land in which you are; for blood pollutes the land and no expiation can be

Looking for Love in the Wrong Place

made for the land for the blood that is shed on it, except by the blood of him who shed it.

Word Study

The Hebrew word for *blood avenger* and *kinsman* is *ga'al,* meaning "to redeem, i.e. to be the next of kin (and as such to buy back a relative's property, marry his widow, etc.) avenger, deliver, (do, perform the part of near, next) kinsfolk (-man), purchase, ransom, redeem (-er), revenger."

The blood avenger, or kinsman redeemer, was to put the murderer to death in payment of life for life. Who is the murderer? Mark the murderer in John 8:44.

John 8

⁴⁴ You are of your father the devil, and you want to do the desires of your father. He was a murderer from the beginning, and does not stand in the truth because there is no truth in him. Whenever he speaks a lie, he speaks from his own nature, for he is a liar and the father of lies.

Read and underline what happens to the Devil and when.

1 John 3

⁸ The one who practices sin is of the devil; for the devil has sinned from the beginning. The Son of God appeared for this purpose, to destroy the works of the devil.

Bushels of Love

What happened to rulers and authorities at the cross of Jesus? Underline the point.

Colossians 2

13 When you were dead in your transgressions and the uncircumcision of your flesh, He made you alive together with Him, having forgiven us all our transgressions,

14 having canceled out the certificate of debt consisting of decrees against us, which was hostile to us; and He has taken it out of the way, having nailed it to the cross.

15 When He had disarmed the rulers and authorities, He made a public display of them, having triumphed over them through Him.

What happened to the devil through the death of Jesus? Underline the point.

Hebrews 2

14 Therefore, since the children share in flesh and blood, He Himself likewise also partook of the same, that through death He might render powerless him who had the power of death, that is, the devil,

In John 8: The Devil is the murderer.

In 1 John 3:8: Jesus came to destroy the works of the Devil.

Looking for Love in the Wrong Place

In Colossians 2:13-15: Jesus made a public display of them, having triumphed over them.

In Hebrews 2:14: Jesus rendered the Devil powerless.

Jesus, our kinsman redeemer, executed the murderer, stripped him of any power over believers, totally disarmed all rulers and authorities, making them a public display, and finally destroyed the Devil's works. So while the thief came to kill, steal, and destroy (John 10), that does not include believers, unless a believer gives him place or opportunity (Eph. 4:27). Remember, John 10:10, Jesus came that we might have abundant life. Our Redeemer lives!

The fascinating love story of Ruth and Boaz turns into a beautiful word picture in the Old Testament that illustrates the dramatic truths of the Christian faith that we find in the New Testament. The story behind the story reveals Christ, our kinsman redeemer, willing and able to radically change our lives. This is our redemption story. It is the ultimate love story.

Read the following passage, making a list of what you learn about the love of God. Mark the words *love* and *hearts*.

Romans 5

⁵ And hope does not disappoint, because the love of God has been poured out within our hearts through the Holy Spirit who was given to us.

Bushels of Love

⁶ For while we were still helpless, at the right time Christ died for the ungodly.
⁷ For one will hardly die for a righteous man; though perhaps for the good man someone would dare even to die.
⁸ But God demonstrates His own love toward us, in that while we were yet sinners, Christ died for us.

How is God's love given to us?

_____

_____

_____

What was our condition at the time?

_____

_____

_____

How did God demonstrate His love to us?

_____

_____

_____

Mark the words *love, separate, God,* and *Christ* in this passage.

Looking for Love in the Wrong Place

Romans 8

³⁵ Who will separate us from the love of Christ? Will tribulation, or distress, or persecution, or famine, or nakedness, or peril, or sword?

³⁶ Just as it is written, "For your sake we are being put to death all day long; we were considered as sheep to be slaughtered."

³⁷ But in all these things we overwhelmingly conquer through Him who loved us.

³⁸ For I am convinced that neither death, nor life, nor angels, nor principalities, nor things present, nor things to come, nor powers,

³⁹ nor height, nor depth, nor any other created thing, will be able to separate us from the love of God, which is in Christ Jesus our Lord.

Who or what can separate us from the love of God?

_____

_____

_____

What are the things that can be conquered because of His love?

_____

_____

_____

Bushels of Love

Selah…Think about it.

1. Did you see the story behind the story? Boaz was Ruth's kinsman redeemer. Jesus was born in the same line and became the kinsman redeemer of the world. Ruth enjoyed the love, protection, provision, and wealth of Boaz. Ask yourself honestly if you are enjoying and walking in the love, protection, provision, and wealth of your Kinsman Redeemer? If so, can you explain how?

   _____

   _____

   _____

2. What did you discover about God's love for you, and how did it relate to Boaz's love for Ruth?

   _____

   _____

   _____

3. Explain how Jesus executed our murderer, and describe the believer's relationship to Satan.

   _____

   _____

   _____

Looking for Love in the Wrong Place

4. Christ fulfilled the criteria of the kinsman redeemer set forth in the Old Testament passages. Are you living a redeemed life, free from the power and penalty of sin? Are you looking for and hastening the coming day of redemption?

   _____

   _____

   _____

5. What lessons have you learned as a result of this study?

   _____

   _____

   _____

This would be a good time to pause and pray, to praise and to thank God for Jesus, our Redeemer.

Appendix

ABSOLUTELY SURE

1 John 5

¹³ These things I have written to you who believe in the name of the Son of God, so that you may know that you have eternal life.

How can you know if you have eternal life? Is it dependent on church attendance, church work, water baptism, growing up in a Christian home, or being a good person? Actually, none of the above! The Word of God says if you have the Son you have life (1 John 5:11-12) and you can know that you know Him if you keep His commands (1 John 2:2-3). Your life, your consistent practice of His word, is the proof of salvation. So, are you saved? How do you know?

Looking for Love in the Wrong Place

Follow the instructions below to see how the Word describes those "born of God" and how you can know if you know Him. Do you line up with the Word?

Read 1 John (all five chapters).

Mark (underline or circle) every occurrence of *born of God* and *know* or *known*.

Make a list of what you discover about those "born of God" and what you can *know* in the spaces provided:

Born of God

1 John 2:29 _____

_____

1 John 3:9-10 _____

_____

1 John 4:7-8 _____

_____

1 John 5:1 _____

_____

1 John 5:4 _____

_____

Appendix: Absolutely Sure

1 John 5:18 _____

_____

I can know...

1 John 2:11 _____

_____

1 John 3:1-2 _____

_____

1 John 3:5-6 _____

_____

1 John 3:14-16 _____

_____

1 John 3:19 _____

_____

1 John 3:22-24 _____

_____

1 John 4:2 _____

_____

Looking for Love in the Wrong Place

1 John 4:6 _____

_____

1 John 4:8 _____

_____

1 John 4:13 _____

_____

1 John 4:16 _____

_____

1 John 5:2 _____

_____

1 John 5:14-16 _____

_____

1 John 5:18-20 _____

_____

Now that you see God's description of those "born of God," and you have made a list of what you can *know,* are you absolutely sure that you are saved? If so, praise the Lord! If not, and you want to be saved, please read on.

Appendix: Absolutely Sure

If you are not saved, if you are still looking for contentment and love in the wrong place, here is how you can be saved so you can get your focus on God and off your circumstances.

1. Believe you are a sinner.

"For all have sinned and fall short of the glory of God."
—Romans 3:23

2. Believe you deserve to go to hell.

"Therefore, just as through one man sin entered into the world, and death through sin, and so death spread to all men, because all sinned."
—Romans 5:12

3. Believe Jesus died to pay for your sins.

"But God demonstrates His own love toward us, in that while we were yet sinners, Christ died for us."
—Romans 5:8

4. Trust Jesus as your Lord and Savior.
   (Romans 10:9-13) that if you confess with your mouth Jesus as Lord, and believe in your heart that God raised Him from the dead, you will be saved; for with the heart a person believes,

Looking for Love in the Wrong Place

resulting in righteousness, and with the mouth he confesses, resulting in salvation. For the Scripture says, "WHOEVER BELIEVES IN HIM WILL NOT BE DISAPPOINTED." For there is no distinction between Jew and Greek; for the same Lord is Lord of all, abounding in riches for all who call on Him; for "WHOEVER WILL CALL ON THE NAME OF THE LORD WILL BE SAVED."

Now is the time to make your decision. Now is the accepted time. Now is the day of salvation!

God is love. Look for love in Him.

BIBLIOGRAPHY

Merriam-Webster, I. *Merriam-Webster's Collegiate Dictionary.* Includes index. (10th ed.). Merriam-Webster: (Springfield, Mass., U.S.A. 1966, c1993.)

Strong, James. *The Exhaustive Concordance of the Bible:* (electronic ed.) Woodside Bible Fellowship. Ontario 1996.

Wuest, Kenneth S. *Wuest's Word Studies from the Greek New Testament:* for the English reader. Eerdmans: Grand Rapids 1997, c1984.

Looking for Love in the Wrong Place

Books and CDs by Jannie M. Wilcoxson:
Books
The "Word" on Health and Nutrition
Let Not your Heart be Troubled
Let My People Go
Thy Word—A Lamp

CDs:
- "So You Say You Are in Love"
- "God's Purpose, My Plan"
- "Knowing God"
- "Jude (Studying Inductively)"
- "Hope for the Depressed"
- "Woman, Have You Been with Jesus?"
- "Forgetting, Pressing, Reaching"
- "Living in the Power of His Resurrection"
- "Nutrition and Health"
- "Word Up: The Power of His Name"

For additional information on tapes, CDs, videos, or books, contact:

Sound Words
PO Box 2105
Dayton, OH 45401-2105
www.soundwords1.org

To order additional copies of

LOOKING FOR

IN THE
WRONG PLACE

Have your credit card ready and call

Toll free: (877) 421-READ (7323)

or order online at: www.winepressbooks.com